Encouraging Signs

ALSO BY RUPERT M. LOYDELL

POETRY
Wildlife (Shearsman Books, 2011)
The Fantasy Kid (Salt Publishing, 2010)
Boombox (Shearsman, 2009)
Lost in the Slipstream (Original Plus, 2009)
An Experiment in Navigation (Shearsman, 2008)
Ex Catalogue (Shadow Train, 2006)
The Smallest Deaths (bluechrome, 2006)
A Conference of Voices (Shearsman, 2004)
Familiar Territory (bluechrome, 2004)
The Museum of Light (Arc Publications, 2003)

COLLABORATIONS
A Music Box of Snakes [with Peter Gillies]
             (The Knives Forks and Spoons Press, 2010)
Serviceable Librettos for the Deaf [with Nathan Thompson]
             (Champagne Troglodyte, 2010)
Memos to Self [with Nathan Thompson] (Underhand Behavior, 2009)
Overgrown Umbrellas [with Peter Dent] (Lost Property, 2008)
Risk Assessment [with Robert Sheppard] (Damaged Goods, 2006)
Make Poetry History [with Luke Kennard] (Miraculous Breath Books, 2006)
Shaker Room [with Lee Harwood] (Transignum, 2005)
Snowshoes Across the Clouds [with Robert Garlitz] (Stride, 2004)
Eight Excursions [with David Kennedy]
             (The Cherry On The Top Press, 2003)
The Temperature of Recall [with Sheila E. Murphy] (Trombone Press, 2002)
A Hawk into Everywhere [with Roselle Angwin] (Stride, 2001)

EDITOR
Smartarse (The Knives Forks and Spoons Press, 2011)
From Hepworth's Garden Out (Shearsman, 2010)
Troubles Swapped for Something Fresh (Salt, 2009)
Voices for Kosovo (Stride, 1999)
My Kind Of Angel: i.m. William Burroughs
             (A Stride Conversation Piece, 1998)

Encouraging Signs

interviews, essays & conversations

Rupert M Loydell

Shearsman Books

First published in the United Kingdom in 2013 by
Shearsman Books Ltd
50 Westons Hill Drive
Emersons Green
BRISTOL
BS16 7DF

Shearsman Books Ltd Registered Office
30–31 St. James Place, Mangotsfield, Bristol BS16 9JB
(this address not for correspondence)

ISBN 978-1-84861-299-0
First Edition

Contents

Encouraging Signs

i.m. Brian Louis Pearce and Dennis Milner,

and for Tony Lopez, Phil Terry & Robert Sheppard:

five of the best teachers anyone could have.

Author's Note

This collection of interviews and essays is only one of many possible books that I could have compiled from my files. Other versions might have included selections focussing on the visual arts (particularly painting), the arts & spirituality, music, teaching and pedagogy, or an anthology of book and/or music reviews. There are two texts I was sorry to not include and would like to point the reader to. The first is a sprawling and in-depth interview by Dee Rimbaud which is posted on his website, the second a dialogue with Mike Ferguson about schools and creative writing, first published in NAWE's *Writing in Education* magazine, and more recently re-published on the Salt books website. Thanks to Dee and Mike, and also to the many other interviewees who have not been included.

I see this work as part of my poetics, which Robert Sheppard has previously articulated as tentative and ever-changing; work of many sorts that is useful to critical and creative thought and practice. I hope it may be as useful to the reader as it has been and remains for me.

I have in the main resisted the temptation to edit, although I have corrected errors and occasionally cut parts of longer interviews. I have also sometimes retitled (or titled) the pieces, and in one or two instances added short introductory passages. These are within square brackets; introductions are otherwise original.

I would like to thank all those who gave permission for interviews to be republished, and for their kindness in originally undertaking them. I would also like to thank the publishers who originally published them: Patricia Oxley, Alistair Fitchett, Jeffrey Side, Peter Samson, George Ttoouli, and the editors of *Geometer*, *Third Way* and *Golden Handcuffs Review*. However, the biggest thanks of all must go to Tony Frazer at Shearsman for agreeing to publishing this book and for patiently helping to shape and edit it.

Place is an Emotion

RUPERT LOYDELL TALKS TO ALAN GARNER

Up the muddy track, through a field full of cows. The gate is opened by a smiling Alan Garner, who leads me to his kitchen. We sit at the table and after a cup of coffee I start the questions.

RUPERT LOYDELL: *You seem to have gone in a circle, from children's books, through more complex [adult?] books, back to even simpler children's books. Can you explain the process?*

ALAN GARNER: That is a view expressed by outside readers. None of my books were written specifically for children, although they understand what I'm saying far more readily. It was originally the publishers who published me as a children's writer.

Red Shift *produced very polarised reactions, people hate it or love it.*

I agree. I've found that the book is in the potentially unhappy situation of being a cult book. Once a book is finished, that's it. I want to be clear of it, to get the writing finished. It's analogous with birth. I don't enjoy the process. People accuse me of trying to be baffling, but I simply want to make the reader contribute to the story.

You've beaten me to it. I wanted to ask you about your statement "I leave the reader gaps to fill in". Does it annoy you when they don't, or when they get it wrong?

The reader can't get it wrong. Every reaction is unique, despite resulting from a permanent text. Interpretation is individual. I find people react to things not deliberately written in. For instance, back in 1963, when *The Moon of Gomrath* was out I met a publisher's rep. [I have time for them: if they don't sell the books in their car boots, I don't eat!] He was enthusiastic about the book, and recalled he'd had sleepless nights over one passage. As he talked about it I thought I knew which passage he meant. I was wrong. It turned out to be a link paragraph that I'd rushed over to get to the next "purple passage". Things like that have resulted in me consciously believing in creative reading. Imaginative, not didactic.

Was the paring down of Red Shift *a technical device, or a very emotive process?*

It presented itself that way. I'll explain my writing process: There is a moment when a conceptual idea stands naked. Something is a book. There is a gap, and then a second moment happens. A book starts to appear. I often write, completely spontaneously, the last paragraph of a book. I don't always understand it, but I know it's the ending. Then the rest of the book appears—sounds and sights, at first out of focus. Then suddenly, it all synchronises, the form included. Once it's finished I start an analytical process. Very little gets altered.

With *Red Shift* the first conceptual point was when someone from Mow Cop was relating a tale passed down to her by her illiterate grandmother. She told of the Romans marching Spanish prisoners through Cheshire, on their way to make a wall. She used this to explain why the people of Mow Cop look foreign. Historically that's inaccurate, but the idea of the "lost Ninth" excited me. That was in 1965. In April '66 I missed a train and sat on a railway platform for an hour, reading graffiti. "Not really now not anymore" suddenly associated itself with Mow Cop. Then there were four or five years of note taking. Barthomley tied in early on—the odd wording of the massacre report attracted my attention. Then the writing came. It was not intellectually possible for me to create the interplay of *Red Shift*. It would be wrong for me to have invented and forced something like that. It happened. I only noticed, or had pointed out, a lot of the word play, repetition, and association, afterwards.

How did The Guizer *fit in? It has been suggested that it explained* Red Shift*?*

It was just what interested me at the time. Although you have to question what produced that interest at that particular time.

Is it a continuation of what you were saying in your essay 'Inner Time'?

Perhaps. With hindsight… probably.

Do you just use myth as a springboard, or is it deeper than that? Are you scared of the myths associated with your books sidetracking the reader, or do they add to the story?

Yes, they do add to the story. Real myth is part of the collective soul, it has no one original author. It is highly charged material that has been worked on, worked over, many, many times. If you use the material in the right way your writing will work. If you get it wrong it will work against you.

I am not responsible for what people find if they work back into myths. I have a lot of contacts with the mythic due to strong research. It puts off the horrible business of actually writing, and I think due to my academic upbringing I can convince myself I'm not skiving! Seriously though, extensive research becomes a foundation for intuitive decisions taken in the actual writing later on.

Red Shift, *I know, took a long time to write. What about the Stone books?*

There was no research—except 43 years of family!

Are The Fairy Tales of Gold *original or re-telling/paraphrase?*

They were written as original, but later I could see the sources I'd drawn on. Each story took about four hours to write, yet I felt quite ill afterwards. It was like using a coffee-grinder plugged straight into the National Grid, with no power step-down. I couldn't write any more for quite a while afterwards. At the moment I'm working on similar, yet more substantial texts.

Are fairy tales as important as myths?

They're very important. They are de-sacrilised myth, and very dangerous things to handle. They are not for children—they got this association, became "nursery tales", in the 19th century with Land and Jacob's re-tellings. They were criticised at the time, but their work became very popular.

Do you have lots of unfinished work, or do you concentrate everything into one end project?

Usually one thing at a time, although things do overlap. I can be writing one thing and researching another.

Can you tell me anything about any new projects that are under way?

I find I can't talk about what hasn't been yet. The first conceptual moment for the next novel [I think it's going to be a novel] was in December 1974. The second moment was in October '79. I still don't know what the story's about!

The film Lamaload, *about the drowned village, I thought was awful. What were you trying to say?*

It was part of a series trying to make place as important as characters. I think you have to realise television doesn't always have to be profound, it can tell anecdotes.

How much did you have to do with the film of Red Shift?

A lot. I don't enjoy making films—I still encounter the problem I discussed in 'Inner Time'. *Red Shift* had an excellent producer, a man called David Rose. He wanted to make the film. We met, and he later chose John Mackenzie as director; I met with John and we discussed the book. We both have different obsessions with violence which is interesting. Over a period of 18 months the script was re-written three times. Adaptation interests me greatly. People who are faithful to a book, or try and extract dialogue, always face great problems. There was some apprehension about using a well known face for Jan, but she was an excellent character actress. The boy who played Tom was facing his first television part. He was having to cope with having to just be someone, not being able to work into a part as in stage work. I tend not to worry about these sort of problems too much. I'm glad the far more problematic preliminary work is done. We shot nearly 200 minutes of film, all that I'd scripted. John then spent six months editing down to the required 90 minutes, producing the film we both wanted. The onus was on the editing. I think the credits said it all—"a film by Alan Garner and John Mackenzie".

What do you think of A Fine Anger?

It scared me because he got so much right. It started out because Neil Philips asked me to check, on a factual level, a chapter about me in his thesis. When he went he left me the chapter to read. I was amazed because he'd correctly inferred all my sources!

Later, when my publishers were discussing some sort of critical analysis of my work I said that he was the only person I knew who could manage it in any capacity. I don't think anyone involved in children's writing and criticism could cope. So Collins commissioned him. He came up for three days and had free access to my cellar full of resource material. I was out all day, so there was no conversation about the book. I don't even know what he looked at. *A Fine Anger* is very personal. There was one bit I asked him to take out, but otherwise it's okay although I don't always see what he's getting at. Afterwards we got to know each other quite well, but it wasn't written as a friend.

So it wasn't like Keith Sagar's book on Ted Hughes where he got to know him on a personal level as well?

No, totally different. It's funny you should mention Ted Hughes—our lives are terribly connected. I'm always bumping into people he's worked with, from technicians through to Gordon Cross whom I work with in a musical capacity. I think in a few decades, looking back, people will regard Alan Garner and Ted Hughes as two [very different] sides to the same coin. Working in the same areas, from different viewpoints.'

I'm fascinated by your statement of intent with regard to faith/belief, to "report the view from here". Couldn't belief stay at the same point whilst you risked, made a commitment?

My belief is underdeveloped compared with my knowledge. I get asked "if you know, why can't you commit?" I find most formal religions concentrate on a certain reality, and narrow vision. I don't want my wide-angle vision blinkered. The church has rather cut itself off from the arts. It isolates Christianity from amongst the mythical, yet it belongs there. Myth adds, not detracts from things like Christ's divinity. It fascinates me that he continued a long history of people being hung on trees to die. I had a fascinating discussion with two priest friends, very different people. I said my belief was a problem, yet they regard it as a buffer against problems. Belief should result in open mindedness, not the opposite.

|

You've said "words were originally poetic". Do you deduce this from the minstrels, from oral histories, folk tales?

Oral, yes, but further back than you've suggested. Something akin to what William Golding's getting at in *The Inheritors*. I was trained as a classicist, and if you study words as a science you find words do not define what they name. They approach it at a tangent, and open up a certain area of mystery.

Something as basic as the experiment Hughes tried with Orghast?

Yes.

Can you tell me about your illustrators? Recently there's been Michael Foreman, and a long time before that Charles Keeping illustrated Elidor.

Charles Keeping complained that he had no holes to fill in *Elidor*, that he could only depict what was already there. He was right. Now I don't feel a novel needs illustrations. With the fairy tales I knew at least fifty per cent would be illustrations. I'm very pleased with Michael's work. I think we have the same emotional, or physic background, although we had very different upbringings. The more complex tales I'm writing at present will have smaller illustrations, more like decorative borders really.

Do you have an illustrator in mind?

Oh—no ideas as yet.

What are your influences?

Nothing major beyond what I use as my resources. Something very important though, not as an intellectual concept, but on a personal level, something I've found—place is an emotion.

[*Stride* 8, 1983]

Strange Mental States

Rupert Loydell talks to Russell Hoban

[At the time of the following interview, *Riddley Walker* had just been adapted for the stage and shown at the Royal Exchange Theatre, Manchester. It got critically slated but I and many others found it a wonderful piece of dramatisation which clarified much of the book. I spotted Russell Hoban at one of the performances we attended and asked him for an interview, which he kindly agreed to. The interview was conducted at his Fulham house in March 1986.]

RUPERT LOYDELL: *I wondered how you felt at the moment, having to go back to* Turtle Diary, *when you were dealing with the film, and* Riddley Walker *for the play?*

RUSSELL HOBAN: Oh, *Turtle Diary* I didn't have anything to do with! That was simply a matter of doing a deal with United British Artists and approving Harold Pinter as screen writer. That was all; I had no further say in the matter.

Pinter didn't come to you?

I saw the film company and they came up with Pinter. Then he came over here to look at the neighbourhood, because it was one of the locations for *Turtle Diary*. He then did the screenplay in three or six weeks—a very short time.

And you did Riddley Walker *in five weeks?*

I did *Riddley Walker* in a year; there were about five weeks of rehearsals.

Did the actors contribute much, or was it very much you objectively? Was there improvisation?

Oh no, there wasn't any improvisation. I mean, Braham Murray was the director, and he very generously allowed me to be at all the rehearsals, and to say anything I wanted to say and to make comments about the text; often there were misinterpretations of the text which I had to correct. The actors didn't put any improvisation into it, beyond what actors normally do, that is as people grouped on stage would work things out. But I must say that the actors did put a very high degree of commitment into it. They consistently put in time above and beyond the call of duty and had meetings where the actors who had either no lines, or only a few lines to speak, worked out their backgrounds and the details of their lives.

I liked the dogs. I wondered when you decided to personify Auntie, and if you thought that worked?

Well, Auntie is spoken of in the book that way—as a person.

But it is much more abstract.

Yes, and on stage the female part is much amplified—it's expanded from what it was in the book. It simply grew—there wasn't any doubt that I wanted her that way, because she was an important aspect of the female principle in the book.

So you wrote it as more of a person than I read in the book, because I always saw it as a more abstract female mother figure.

Well, in the book they talk about Auntie as the Death Figure—when you die you need a death figure to step in. My reference for this was a hag figure in Indian religion; the idea of the hag as an aspect of the Mother Goddess occurs in many mythologies throughout the world, and seemed important.

Beyond the Saint Eustace story there seemed very few remnants of Christianity, or Western religions. Do you think they wouldn't survive?

Well, I was making the assumption that, after the destruction of civilisation by nuclear bombs or by nuclear technology—either way—in a few thousand years Christianity might well have fallen by the wayside, simple because people would turn against anything that had brought them to that point of destruction. They would have turned against the technology that did it, they would have turned against any religion involved in the build up to it.

At Riddley Walker, *there were a lot of confused people. The first time I went I ended up, as the only one who had read the book, in a group of people trying to explain it. Does that worry you, or do you just think people should see it again and talk about it?*

It bothers me there's nothing I can do about it. When I wrote the book, I write it the way it came to me, and I took a lot of trouble with it. I spent five and a half years getting it right. When I was satisfied that I had got it right, I considered it finished. Now, with the stage play, it was the same thing. I had to make a highly concentrated version of the material in the book, and I went through nine drafts before rehearsals started. I really worked it into a tenth draft during rehearsals, with many cuts and changes. There, too, I thought that I had finally got it right, I had Braham Murray's comments all through the drafts, and he and I both thought it worked by the time we got to the final copy.

I don't believe, as you say, in writing down to people. There is some material that is by its nature difficult, and if you make it easy, all you are doing is draining the material of its vitality. There is no way to make everything easy.

You often use the theme of something living behind our eyes. Is that something you actually believe or just a literary device?

No, I actually feel it. It is more than a matter of belief—it just feels that way to me, as if we are inhabited by something that lives with us.

Does that tie in with your interest in shamanism?

I suppose so, in that shamanism is a mode of opening the self, opening the conscience, to forces that we can't ordinarily perceive in ordinary ways. In my writing I am always trying to be more open to things that don't come to our minds in ordinary states, and the way I do it is just by tuning in obsessively to ideas that come to me, by working late at night, by staying with things until I am very tired, and until this stiffness of the mind breaks down and loosens up, and thoughts come in that wouldn't come.

That is a sort of sensory deprivation almost, where you stay until you are tired—ready for writing. Have you looked at the surrealist, automatic writers, that sort of thing?

No, which ones do you mean?

The surrealists believed that—basically they did what you did. They wrote from the subconscious. Artaud is one who wrote then; he founded the Theatre of the Absurd.

Going on from that, do you see yourself as anything more than a storyteller, as a modern shaman? Is that too strong a word?

No, I don't think that is too strong a word. That is the novelist's proper function, well as I see it—there are all kinds of novelist, and that is the kind I am. I get into all kinds of strange mental states, and I invite ideas that are not what we ordinarily entertain.

Do you see it as cathartic, for you?

Yes, it is cathartic for me, but I think that it is useful to society in general to have people who do that, because I think that our—what I would call our "limited reality consensus", what we call our normal idea of reality, isn't very useful, it isn't much good. It is like a road map that doesn't have most of the roads on it.

I wondered how interested you are in telepathy, psychic phenomena, things which we are taught to be very sceptical about?

I have always been interested in that kind of thing since childhood. I remember we had a book in the house called Mental Radio, by a writer who is not normally associated with that kind of thing, Upton Sinclair, and I also remember writing to J.P. Riley of Duke University, who sent me a set of cards and things about his ESP experience. I have always felt that the mind has faculties that don't ordinarily come into use, and cannot be controlled by us, but they are there.

And does that tie in with Riddley Walker, Pilgermann *and* The Lion…?

I was going to answer *Jachin-Boaz and Boaz-Jachin*, just ordinarily.

You talk about "doers", and suggest to Riddley that he should be called Riddley Runner instead of Walker. Is it doers who control their destiny, rather than us being controlled by something behind our eyes?

Well, I didn't, I called Riddley a "happener" in the book, not a doer, this being an active person. Do I think they control their destiny? I don't know that I think of anybody controlling his or her destiny. I think more of us living out what is in us to be lived out, living out the action that comes to us, living out the action that enters us.

Which is where Riddley gets caught up, running round.

Yes, he is doing what nations are doing now. They are caught up in this action because it is the sort of action that catches you up.

I wondered if that was why I noticed in the play the mention of Cruise, which I don't think is in the book, but it became very direct. Was that deliberate, to bring it home?

It was deliberate.

What about the sexual aspect, does that just derive from mythology, which is often fairly free?

Which sexual aspect?

Well, you've got Auntie at death being seen in copulation, and in Pilgermann *there is a lot of sexual violence.*

I think that humankind is tremendously violent, and is obviously much motivated by sex. The idea of death being an experience where you do it with Auntie… I hadn't ever found that in any mythology; it seemed right to me as being part of the natural cycle, that death is a coupling of the self with that aspect of the Great Mother that swallows you up, uses you and finishes you off.

Do you think Riddley Walker *offers us any hope? A lot of people thought it was pessimistic, although I saw it as the characters getting to a new stage.*

I think it is a very optimistic book. It has in it the idea that although we are driven by all sorts of demons that make us destroy ourselves, we are equally driven by demons that make us try to understand why we destroy ourselves. So in us there is always a mingling of destructive and creative forces. I don't think that humankind has ever worked out whether it wants to live or die. It is always assumed that we want to live, but our actions do not bear them out, because what we do with cars on the roads, what we do with drink, what we do with drugs, with cigarettes, what we do with violence everywhere…

It does not look as if we are actually certain which it is we want, and I don't think that this has ever been recognised. It is always assumed that we really do want to live, and I don't think we can make that assumption. I think the two urges are always in conflict, and the conflict is still unresolved.

So that is a very important thing that you try to put across in art? You think art is the place to try and show people?

Yes. I think it is not so much a didactic thing, trying to show people something, although you are trying to show them something. The artist is a respondent. In one way and another the artist takes in the world coming at him, and responds to it in what he does, and I think any full response will have in it the recognition of that mingled urge to kill humankind and to keep it living.

You would like to show people the options they have got rather than expect anything—without preaching?

In effect one is showing. What I am simply doing is responding to what I am compelled to respond to. I don't have any choice in the matter. This is what comes at me and I am not able to do anything but what I'm doing.

Can you tell us how you actually write? You said you stay up late to push a response. Do you push a response along a story line, a theme, or around an object?

Well, I have a very simple discipline. I work seven days a week. I start writing after breakfast, and I work all morning. I have a nap after lunch, then I work in the afternoon, in the late evening and late at night, so on my full strength days it is usual to put in ten hours or so. I simply stay with the thing until it lets go of me. It is as simple as that.

You reject a lot. Do you keep it on file?

I reject a lot, but I keep it around. I use a word processor, so I have it on a disc. But it takes me a long time to get things down on paper the way I want them, and very often I'll spend a whole day over a paragraph, or a whole page, and then find it's nothing I can use after all.

I know you edited 500 pages from Riddley.

Well, that was the first two years of it, which I just discarded.

Will you ever… will that end up as part of another book, or is it just by-product?

No, it won't end up as part of another book.

I must admit that Pilgermann, *although I'm in the middle of reading it again, left me very confused.*

Which surprises me.

Is Jewish theology important to you? Were you brought up in the faith?

No, I was not brought up as a practising Jew. I stayed home from school on Jewish holidays, but that was about the extent of it. Before I wrote *Riddley Walker* I didn't know that I was going to spend five-and-a-half years dealing with what the bomb is in our lives, and before I wrote *Pilgermann* I didn't realise I was going to become immersed in Judaism and Islam and Christianity, as I had to be when I wrote that. Things come to me and take over, and I have to go with them. For *Pilgermann* I brought a tremendous number of books, borrowed from the reference library, and had to sit down and read all kinds of things of which I was ignorant.

Did you enjoy the research bit?

I did, yes. Research is always enjoyable, it's very easy to let research become a stall, and you can put off ever writing the book by just researching and researching.

I wondered if you had ever read Alan Garner, as I spoke to him a couple of years ago, and he basically said he's got the same writing process as you. he researched Red Shift *for five years—which was Roman History in Cheshire— and put off writing for as long as possible, then got down to it for two years.*

I have only read *The Owl Service*, and not *Red Shift*, and I didn't research *Riddley Walker* for five years. I was working on it for five years, and the research on it wasn't all that much. For *Pilgermann* I was working for two years, and I don't remember how much of that time was reading and research.

Would you mind saying something about what Pilgermann *means to you, without giving the game away?*

It's funny, you would think somebody would have asked me that before but nobody has, and I haven't got a prepared statement in my mind.

But you must see it as more than a series of Bosch-like images and things about different theologies?

Yes, it is more than that, but I could not define what it is. You know I always write without a plan, without an outline. When people ask me what I had in mind I am always reminded of an interview somewhere with Buster Keaton, where the interviewer said "In such and such a scene"—whatever it might have been, in this train chase or something like that—"was this symbolising the conflict between capitalism and the workers?" or whatever, some high-flying question. And he said, "No, what we do is work out one scene, then work out another scene." And that is about what I do. I always go by how it feels and how the thing takes me. I always think of it as flying by the seat of my pants. If it feels right, if it feels as if it's going right, as if the thing is finding the shape that it wants, and getting itself down on paper the way that it wants, I trust that it means something.

Certainly, looking back, Riddley *is about events after "the bomb". It is obviously a lot more than that, but there is nothing that just stands out.*

I couldn't really say there is.

I wondered about the idea of personification in Kleinzeit. *Was it just a literary device? I mean, it is very funny, and it is interesting how it makes the characters work against it.*

Russell Hoban

Well, my answer to that is that things are always talking to us in one way or another. A simple example of this is a hard chair with a straight back is saying "sit up straight", and a deeply upholstered easy chair says "sink back and relax"; a narrow pavement says "you have to walk in single file", and a broad walk says "you can walk side by side". Everything is talking in one way or another. I always experience the world as being animistic. Things are speaking personally to me.

Did you write it as humorous? It comes over as incredibly funny.

Oh sure, purposely.

I think you have stopped writing for children?

Well, I haven't done it for a long time.

Did you enjoy writing for children at the time?

I still do, but I have not had any commercially successful children's books since some of the very early ones—the Frances books. Now I have done a number of books called *Bedtime for Friends, Bread and Jam for Friends*, this and that for friends... And those were all done more than twenty years ago.

So things like the crocodile, which I have got, haven't sold well?

You mean *Dinner at Alberta's*? No, they haven't. The ones that have sold well are of a particular kind. They are always didactic, they always deal with a little domestic conflict of some kind that is humorously and plausibly resolved.

A couple of years ago you wrote an article for The Listener, *reviewing the TV programme* Threads. *It is always unfair to quote, but there you said "Hell is where we are". Do you mean that you are living in some kind of hell, or do we create one?*

That was a quote from Marlowe. Dr Faustus says "Hell is where we are", and I simply mean—Heaven is where we are too—this is where it is all happening. This is the depth of our despair, and our punishment, right now is the punishment for our sins, and right now is the reward for ever.

So you don't believe in a personal God? Just this abstract thing?

I believe in the god I think of as "it", this what-ever-it-is that is looking out from the eyeholes in our faces, living in us and making us live out its impulsions.

But there is no give and take, no personal relationship beyond that manipulation?

I don't know... I always feel that we are going on from what Camus says about life being an absurd game. It is an absurd game, but I seem to remember that he also says that it has its rules and one ought to play it honourably. I feel it is on us to respond to what is moving us, by living out our response. [That's not very clear!]

You mean living—"extremely" sounds ridiculous... living life to the full, even in despair, that sort of idea?

It is very difficult to say anything which is an absolutely incomparable logical argument, but in the tragedy of Oedipus, when you watch it I think there is always a lift to the spirits, simply because watching it we feel that Oedipus has made his tragedy his. He is not simply a victim, but he has entered fully into the living out of himself which resulted in his being driven out with blood streaming from his eye sockets. He comes out on top of it, he transcends it, because he takes it into himself and makes it his own. So he ends up as being someone whose burial is though of as giving good luck to the place where he is buried.

This is not any kind of big statement. It is what it is. I think big things that we feel are not really clear arguments of any kind, they are just powerful gut feelings.

So you are living your life to the full by writing; you've got a compulsion to write?

Yes, that's right.

Do you draw any more?

No, I don't. Writing is all I do.

Can you tell us what you are working on at the moment? A continuation of the article in Granta *magazine?*

I am working on what I hope will be my next novel, called *The Medusa Frequency*. That is where the conversation will be more obvious.

And is that excerpt the preface? In your article it said "the preface".

No, it is an episode in the thing. It has gone through a number of revisions so it is not as it was in *Granta*, but it is still a conversation with the Head of Orpheus.

Is there still a narrator in the book?

Yes, there is still a narrator, and [I can't describe it any more than the rest of my books] this has to be do with the action between men and women more than my other books have done.

In an emotional and sexual way?

Yes.

Do you think it is important to almost re-invent myth, which is what you do when you take a Greek myth and weave it into a new story?

Yes, I think the myth-making capability is vital to our survival, and I think it has been allowed to atrophy, to shrivel up. I think the mythic way of receiving things is a natural one, that helps us understand the world better, to get a better grip on things than what you would call the rational.

Are you versed in American myth as well, and English myth, or do you just follow whatever you are interested in?

I don't think there is much myth in America, there is folklore and legend of a kind.

Is that because it is such a young country? What about the Native American Indians?

I used to read Indian references as a child.

Do you read other authors who work with you? What influences you?

No. Most of my reading is either research or light entertainment reading. I don't read other contemporary novelists.

You read classics?

Classics or classical? Classics is like Greek or Latin.

Modern classics I mean.

Yes. I have read all Dickens' novels and most of Trollope.

But not writers of this century? You're not interested in the Americans?

Oh, I've read some of Faulkner... Up to what point have I read modern literature? I guess I would draw the line at live authors. I haven't read many of those. A lot of dead guys, but not too many of the live ones.

So when you use a literary device in your books, you don't read people like Joyce, and look for literary devices—they come to you spontaneously as you write your books?

As far as I know. I haven't read Joyce, well I have read *Portrait of the Artist as a Young Man*, but I never made it with *Ulysses*. I can't remember how many pages I read of it, when I was seventeen or eighteen. I can't think of any writers who influenced me stylistically. I can think of several writers who have shown me standards to work by, so that I can think of the density of Conrad's writing and the way he used all kinds of baffles and screens to keep you circling around the essence of whatever story he was telling; I think of the vitality in Dickens, just the amount of action in his words. I think of the light and shade and colour in Walter de la Mare, and of the three that I've just named I guess that Walter de la Mare is the closest, in that the territory he writes in is pretty much the territory in which I write—that is the shadowy edges of things.

You don't see other living novelists involved in the same myth-making or storytelling that you are?

You see, I don't see them.

I mean, you don't regard them as being.

I have no idea. I'm sure a lot of them are.

You said it was important to carry on myth-making and yet other people who might be doing this, you don't read?

I am sure there are other people doing it. I just don't want to know what they are doing, because one way and another they put me off. I am naturally too competitive, and if somebody else is doing something and I know about it, then it is going to bother me too much.

Do you enjoy being almost a cult? You have become almost a bookish man. Picador is quite a trendy literary publisher.

In my experience, if I am a cult, it means that a lot of people know about me but I don't sell a lot of books.

You would rather be a household name and have more people read your books?

Well, I would rather make a little more money out of it than I do!

[*Stride* 26, 1986]

Redemptive Writing

AN INTERVIEW WITH BRIAN LOUIS PEARCE

[Brian Louis Pearce was a friend of my parents, and one of my first influences with regard to poetry and creative writing; he also became my friend and someone whose work I took great pride and delight in publishing through Stride. (Other titles mentioned below were published by Oasis, Magwood, Outposts and The Quarto Press.) This interview was the final one of four included in a *festschrift* for him, which I edited and published as part of the Stride Research Documents series.]

RUPERT LOYDELL: *In re-reading your earlier work it's clear that around the time of* The Argonauts *you moved away from romantic archaisms into a more contemporary, if still lyrical, realism. What precipitated this?*

BRIAN LOUIS PEARCE: The effect of wide reading, perhaps; particularly Yeats. I was living in the Chilterns c. 1957, with colleague Peter Craddock. The kickstart probably came from his motorbike and the country we leaned through at 45 degrees. 'Coombe Hill', 'Time's Lovers' and 'Paignton Harbour' date from then. 'Epithalamion…' came in 1958, after I returned to London and met the prototype of 'Gillian' in *London Clay*.

Still, looking back to earlier poems, I'd be interested to know how much you felt the form *of your work related to the paintings you wrote about in poems such as 'Thames Below Westminster' (Monet), 'Railway Bridges' (Pisarro) and 'The Telephone in the Desert' (Dali).*

'Telephone…' and 'Thames Below' are very much examples of hitting on a literary or poetic equivalent for the surrealist/impressionist visual images, respectively. I was full of de Chirico at that time, too. In 'The States of Mind' pieces (in *Selected Poems*) it was the juxtaposed content and movement, and the general futurist method of Boccioni to which I responded. Boccioni has three pieces of that title. I added a fourth.

Presumably they're very different to work such as Off Cape Oil—*where you respond to paintings you saw,* Jack o'Lent—*were the 'Heads' paintings were a springboard to a whole sequence on other themes (although starting with six very referential poems), or* Gwen John Talking—*which is more biographical and philosophical?*

30

In the Preface to *Off Cape Oil* I wrote: "A recent postgraduate exhibition at the Slade… disquieted the author so that he gave birth to 'Heads, I lose'; disturbed him into the comment implied in 'Crossing the Line: acrylic'; and excited him, by figures in fine outline, to produce…" (the title poem and others). It's not dissimilar to finding verbal equivalents, but ends up with texts (in the first two cases) that the artist wouldn't have dreamed of. *Jack o'Lent* takes this trend much further. It enters into the expressionist angst and deliberately broken or jagged marks in Bacon's pictures: but as an attempt to work out those things that concerned *me* (the death of an acquaintance; Easter again, and personal emotion) by breaking up words and traditional modes so as to make us feel and hear *from the poems*, a world-view (or questioning) entirely my own; yet not unrelated to what Bacon must have felt. I'd read his interviews. The first half dozen poems do project my own response to his papal screaming heads in glass boxes (after Velázquez). I've implanted Lenten customs in the sequence too (taken from throughout Europe). Fertility rite and redemptive, mitigating acts seems to me interlinked and highly relevant. *Gwen John Talking* attempts to construct a total picture of the painter's emotional and spiritual pilgrimage from her words and life, and my response to (sometimes descriptions of) her pictures. It took a while, just as *Jack…* did. It includes a narrative poem in four sections ('To Dieppe: a lifescape') which builds up her biography and feelings from her own and John Rothenstein's words as well as mine. That again's something different.

You've written several poems about your father since his death, as I have of mine. Was he particularly influential? I see there's another father poem—'Second Coming'—in the new 'City Whiskers' sequence:

> Losing and finding a
> father's not a thing we
> do every day, yet the
> loss goes on every day
> and the search, too

Your father also makes an almost visionary appearance in 'Below'.

Relations with fathers (actual or mythical) can be very intriguing and significant. One thinks of Gosse's *Father and Son* and Virginia Woolf's *To the Lighthouse*, and what Golding says in his 1985 interview with John Carey. Then I got a lot from Isherwood's *Prater Violet*. I wrote quite a few poems before my own father died that are related to him or father-figures. There are several in *The Argonauts* dating from 1957 or 8. 'Boneplace' was written soon after his death, and there are also 'Oedipus' and 'At the Crossroads' in *Selected Poems*. I think I got my sympathy for the underdog, the loser, from him. He was a carpenter, who failed to set up as a builder between the wars; whilst very young he had volunteered for the First War. He read a lot. The more sociable, if equally self-effacing, side of me came from my mother, a civil servant with a wide circle of friends, and a Baptist minister in the family tree, hence some of my earlier editings and attempts at fiction. *Potter's House* has a grandfather figure.

It's remorse, isn't it, partly, this pre-occupation. The wish to still, belatedly, *connect* with them, as well as to have them back. You recall Hardy's poems to Emma Gifford after she'd died, so very heartfelt. My father would have liked me to have taken after him, I expect, yet maybe his carpentry skills—and polishing the bits that aren't seen—are part of my poetry. Fathers come into my fiction quite a lot. There's Victoria Hammersmith's father, and the whole meaning (almost) of *A Man in His Room*, and the relationship between F/Sgt Haines and the narrator in *The Servant of His Country*, where there are other father figures, too. It's an intrinsic part of *The Goldhawk Variations*, and it's the narrator's main difficulty in *The Deacons* really, the need to choose between three (or more) types of father figure, reflecting the rational, emotional, artistic and other strands in his own nature. Then there's the concept of God the Father or of fathers as aspects of God. Whether or not "theologically sound" (your term!) it comes into a lot of my recent poetry. *Jack o'Lent* explores it, and 'Yard's End' (poem 31) specifically stems from my dad's shed. 'Second Coming' stems from my thinking about four or five men known to me—and ties up with a number of other poems in 'City Whiskers'. One's called 'Old Wise Man' you'll see. Yes, he does come back in 'Below'. In that case it picks up from a scene in 'The Hampstead Affair'. Of course, there are other strands in it. There's an old man in *The Bust of Minerva*, too… at the start and finish. Has that been spotted?

How serious are you about this idea of "redemptive writing"? It's hardly theologically sound in any traditional way, is it? Presumable you relate it to the Yeats' quote you use in 'The Old Rogue': "Great literature is the forgiveness of sin"? Does this mean you aspire to writing great literature?

"Redemptive writing"? It's Martin Caseley's phrase... could apply to 'Tessa Black-friars', I think, and to 'Pryde of Islemond' (part of *The Tufnell Triptych*), *Battersea Pete*, the folk in 'The Café at Applegarth Park', and to what I've been writing lately. But I don't think I'd want to make such a claim myself. It's not often conscious or deliberate, for one thing, and difficult to aim at when setting out. It can come as a bonus, though. I write because I can't help it; intuitively, hoping to illuminate an event, person or relationship, and in the hope of shaping a good artefact. Yet the pre-occupation with what Martin is concerned with stems from my whole thought and background subconsciously and the play *Shrine Rites*, for instance, is nothing if not a redemptive act. I'm always trying to understand life and my "theological" position; attempting to find meaning and to fashion some order in the chaos; that's part of why one writes. There's catharsis when one's done it, I suppose. One can go to one's bed "justified", in the theological sense, as I do in the poem 'Eye'. But it's a work of art one's thinking about, not a sermon or treatise. As for aspiring to write great literature, goodness, of course I do. Just as Connolly said we should, and Keats and George Steiner would agree. What else is worth sweating at? That doesn't mean it has to seen dead serious—it can involve the inconsequential too. It's the "forgiveness of sin" I was emphasising in 'The Old Rogue', stemming from Browning and Yeats, not the "great literature" bit. I am a lay preacher, of course; we have to acknowledge that, though I think in the context of my imaginative work it can be misleading. The point is I do not think of art as propaganda, or as the principle vehicle of my ideas; so my beliefs, doubts, feelings, hunches will be there, but implicitly. Think how much fiction is weakened by its rehearsal of ideas, and that goes even more form a poem.

Would you therefore refute A.C. Evans' idea that your characters (and by inference, you) fly into "a sacred world of artistic certainty", away from the modernist "trends in society that have destroyed so many good men of his generation..."?

I *don't* replace (or confuse) God with art, though I have felt the temptation. As for the "sacred" world, I wish I could be a little more certain, but I have come to think that Kierkegaard was right in telling us that we must exist in uncertainty. If I've managed to create a sense of my values—gentleness, consideration, self-restraint, a respect for privacy and individuality and, most precious of all, a sense, however hesitant, of God-with-us—in my writings, I'd be very pleased. There's a "sacred world" of civility that we inherit and can pass on if we choose, and which we can all share. One has to distinguish "modernist" as a literary term—involving many of the authors who I like, and much of what I think I am as a writer—and "modernist" applied to out troubled and permissive society, in which so many received values have disappeared. I write as a doubting believer... a seeker/celebrator of the Divine. "Do you see yonder shining light? I think I do. Then go up toward that." (Bunyan) That's it. And the light's often in those round us, or the things that happen each day.

I want to question you about your idea of "realism". We've spoken about Battersea Pete *before, and you've defended the characters there. Now I want to look at* The Bust of Minerva. *Yann Lovelock suggests that you have sketched a Southerner's jaundiced, cliché Midlands/Northern town, using sweeping assumptions and generalisation, in a way that insults the reader. I have to say that I found the main character totally unbecoming, with his whingeing about 80p cups of tea and the like; I simply wanted to shake him hard and tell him it's the 1990s and that's what tea costs! I'm not sure that he is at all realistic, or if he's an extreme, and definitely not the "everyman" among us. How would you answer these criticisms?*

Let the reader be the judge. There are such things as "personas" and sense of proportion. The narrator enjoyed his Manchester and I think that comes over... its people, places and art. The traveller is looking at the Midlands from the railway line and his view is conditioned by that. He thinks of it as I write elsewhere of Acton or Willesden; other places for which I feel affection. "It was as it was, and he liked it", he says; "didn't want to see it altered." More productive discussion points could have been: How is the piece built up? Does it work as an extended prose poem? Do I successfully (in publisher Ian Robinson's words) use "the framework of a journey to Manchester and the events that take place there as a means to investigate his, or the narrator's, attitude to art and how the recreation in art of lived experience can sometimes render a satisfaction that life does not often provide"?

I don't think I am (or would wish to be) the "everyman" amongst us. Would there be a point in me writing, or you reading, if I was? One *transmutes* experience—if one is capable of it; that's the thing. Giving it "added value" (perish the phrase!), if one is lucky. Yet it's true that one writes not only for oneself, but for those on one's wavelength... and most,

I suppose, in my case, to engage with the private selves of reflective nature. But everyone's welcome to tune in.

'Below' seems to me a very insular kind of story. I enjoy the jokes, puns and actual writing itself, but isn't there a danger that this dense web of private allusion and literary quotes doesn't reach the general reader? Are you, like Colin in the story, more concerned with "the poetry of the thing"?

Yes, but Joyce (and Woolf) made a go of it, here and there, and I can't see why another shouldn't try something related but different. At least my readers are spared his inordinate length! One wants to tell a story, create character, but it's the "poetic" thing that may be my most valuable contribution. What do *you* think? Who *is* this general reader? It's a "visitor's London" anyhow—as someone said of *London Clay*—which most people can pick up. There are one or two allusions to lost rivers, but most of it is a play on everynight social situations. There's evocation of place and atmosphere. The snow… and my Dad again. I like to highlight the glamour of the everyday.

William Oxley has written that he believes you are principally a poet, even when writing your prose—with an ear and an eye for music in words.

Absolutely! That's why one or two of the other questions could be seen as misdirected or over-stated. It explains my pre-occupation with patterning in fiction—that partially repeated passage at the end of 'The Cafe…', for example—and why *Victoria Hammersmith* could come into consideration as my major "poem", though it's full of characters and interest in how they behave. I was writing fiction by the age of twenty, but put it aside. But William is right—it took a poet to see it!—provided the remark is not preclusive.

In 'City Whiskers' you have moved on from Jack o'Lent *to an even denser, but longer-lined, style of syllabic poetry, yet 'The Proper Fuss' sees a return to earlier lyricism, subject, and more traditional poetics. Are you being schizophrenic in your writing, or is the form inherently part of what you want to say? Are you returning to your poetic roots?*

Sometimes one is in the mood of Hughes' *Crow*, sometimes not. *Jack o'Lent* was urgent, as the boy said. 'The Proper Fuss' is far more relaxed, with elegies celebrating Barker, Bacon, Panufnik, and lyrics, happy in mood, syllabic or traditional, responding to summer. 'City Whiskers' is structured strictly, with lots of sound energy—based on London landmarks, but very varied in subject matter, with several serious themes running through it. It's laconic, and accessible, I would have thought. What we're talking about is the application of technique to different problems; exposure of the poetic self to different stimuli as they turn up. One may *plan* a sequence or major work. One may *respond* to unexpected events… a holiday, a death, a meeting. But you ask a good question, which all artists have to go on answering. Whether to go on exploring; to stand still, or to go back? I think one probably wants, and needs, to go on, but I wouldn't criticise anyone for going back, as de Chirico did. One might do that, and then go forward again. *Respiciens, propsiciens* is a good motto.

You seem to have moved in your faith from the full-blooded resurrection and salvation of earlier poems to the low key "whisker of grace" that runs through the city at the end of 'City Whiskers'. Are you more sceptical? More realistic? Doubting? Or what…?

I'm not sure how "full-blooded" I ever was on these questions, but you're right, I suppose about (say) the Easter sequence in *Selected Poems*. I don't like glib or over-assured answers, especially when they coerce our behaviour or beliefs. I'd like to think that I'm more open, and perhaps one becomes humbler as one gets older. More and more I believe that God comes to us individually, and is to be found in many different people and aspects of his creation every day. Yet he is absolute, surely, and not dependent on what *we* think about Him, and the sacraments continue to vouchsafe to us sacred truths, at the heart of our relationship with Him. These two concepts go side by side, and have to be held in balance, I guess. If you go and see something like the display of marine plant life in the Palm House at Kew Gardens, it reminds one once again of the wonder of creation; yet, when someone dies, it is still a struggle to understand what, if anything, remains of them. *Jack o'Lent*, parts of 'City Whiskers' and *The Goldhawk Variations* wrestle with these things.

I'm struck by Murillo's picture *The Two Trinities* in the National Gallery. One imaginary circle encompasses God the Father, Son, and Holy Spirit—the latter represented, in the traditional manner, by a dove. The other takes in Mary and Joseph with Jesus, depicting them as an "ordinary" human family. There's a lot of meaning in that.

Both William Oxley and A.C. Evans write of a suppressed sexuality in your work; suggesting the idea of muse, partner, and "other woman" as recurring themes. Do you accept that? Are there definite sexual undertones written into the work? Clearly the relationships in London Clay *have to work at all levels of reality, including the sexual. Do you accept Freudian or Jungian interpretations of relationships? Do you believe I any relationship with "the Muse"?*

Is it suppressed in my fiction? Ungratified, might be nearer the mark. If people talk about a thing, or acknowledge it to themselves even, it is not suppressed. Perhaps the commentators are simply saying that there is more sexuality than they might have expected, but that it is not of a tabloid nature. It comes back to my background, for sexuality can be gross or refined (as a springboard for refined accord and fruition) and/or sublimated, a word out of fashion today. I would guess most people are subject to both kinds of stimuli, gross *and* refined, for it is one of the chief drives and pleasures/interests/creative forces of life. It is what we do with it that matters. It provides the energy that sets one at one's desk. It makes possible some of the most beautiful, gentle, fructifying relationships (or aspects of relationships) that give meaning and happiness to our lives. It merges into empathy and companionship, the importance of which are quite inadequately recognised. Our use of it depends on, and indicates, the extent to which we are civilised. It ties up with aspiration. That's where "the Muse" comes in. Poets like Yeats, Hardy, Graves, Ratcliffe and Redgrove illustrate that. You'll find all this in my fiction, yes, and in my poetry, right up to my most recent poems. *Gwen John Talking* is worth looking at from this point of view. What sexuality is *not*, for any responsible person, is the assumption that it involves nothing but explicit physical expression. Hence the significance of the creative outlet and labour… and labour is often the appropriate word, going as it does with the idea of inspiration/enthusiasm at conception. It is not for nothing that Hardy's wife said that his work was his "child". I'm not exactly a Jungian, but I find him sympathetic, much more so than Freud.

Are you angry at being ignored by publishers and critics? Or the general public? Has it led to the self deprecation we find in work like 'The Old Rogue'? This poem seems in direct contrast to the clear belief in your own work that I know you hold. Or am I, once again, confusing fiction and poetry with autobiography?

I'd like to think of my work as inspired mischief, but you ask such serious questions of it! 'The Old Rogue' refers to the fellow's "kite of ambition, bumping against the stars". I don't know about the self-deprecation; a wry mask if often worn by my narrators, admittedly. I suppose irony and disguise is an early defence of introspective natures, and the habit sticks. The consequence of the laggard recognition that so many experience, reduces the amount of a writer's *oeuvre* and the extent of what he can produce at his physical and nervous peak. It also denies the reading public's awareness of it, let alone, acquaintance with, the range of writing available, thus perpetuating a lopsided culture, and circumscribing writer and reader alike. It's a pity I think, and apart from my reading of Eliot's *Notes towards the Definition of Culture* I imagine he would have agreed. But there are the economic factors; the deadening concept of the mass market, and (to be fair) the fact that there are so many of us writing today. So the happy writer is the one who enjoys his or her own work!

[*Emotional Geology: the writings of Brian Louis Pearce*, Stride, 1993]

Brian Louis Pearce

Poetic Assessment: John Burnside

John Burnside is a conjurer of mystic moments, an author who captures the transient, the mysterious, and who pushes his work towards transcendence and epiphany. He is a serious and considered writer, strangely out of place among The Young Generation Poets and other media nonsense he has been associated with, best read in old-fashioned quiet, then slowly re-read, savoured and pondered. He is not a difficult writer, but one to be enjoyed, one skilled in all he should be. From *Common Knowledge*—his second book—onwards (I prefer to leave *The Hoop* [Carcanet, 1998] alone as simply a forerunner, a hint of things to come) even the simplest images of his are mysterious and come laden with portent:

> Smoke in the woods
> like someone walking in a silent film
> beside the tracks
> (from 'Signal Stop, Near Horsley')

The poem goes on to conjure the beginning of winter, and compare its arrival to a girl the narrator occasionally glimpses from the train. Throughout the book Burnside draws the reader in with simple language, sometimes directly addressing them:

> Like me, you sometimes waken
> early in the dark
> thinking you have driven miles
> through inward country

> [...]

> Sometimes you linger days
> upon a word,
> a single, uncontaminated drop
> of sound; for days

> it trembles, liquid to the mind,
> then falls:

mere detonation,
dimming in the undertow of language.
    (from 'Home')

This adherence to the "uncontaminated drop", allowing oneself to be caught in "the undertow of language" seems to me central to Burnside's poetry. The poet has something he wants to evoke and is not going to let the language or poem be sidetracked from that task and destination. In *Common Knowledge* (Secker & Warburg, 1991) there are two long prose-poem sequences, one exploring the concept of suburbia, the other the annunciation. They try very hard to be mysterious and moody, but without being silly or trite. They are beautiful, evocative pieces, and there are many more successful poems in 1992's *Feast Days* (also Secker & Warburg). I was less convinced by the next book, The Myth of the Twin (Cape, 1994), where it seemed Burnside tried too hard, and fell into formulaic poetry. He struggled for epiphany but failed, perhaps because the poems seem to contain too much self-doubt: "I almost believe…" he says,

I half-expect a silence I could touch
to form at nightfall over love and prayers
when each soft household folds into the dark.
    (from 'Credo')

Previously, Burnside would have shown us the silence and passed it on to us, palpable and real, conveyed in rich, earthy language, but in this book he seems, as the same poem later says, "tongue-tied and beguiled".

But in 1995's *Swimming in the Flood* (Cape), which contains poems I have heard called pretentious, vague and nasty, Burnside has moved on to a world where he can evoke the dark side of the unknown, conjuring "the quiet erasure of distance" rather than the confirmation of nearness, of good (or God).

Burnside goes looking for epiphany, the transient. He stated:

For the sign I have waited to see
is happening now
and always
    (in 'Parousaia')

but maintains—earlier in the same poem—that "All resurrections are local".

It is this personalised moment, this perhaps selfish kind of evocation, I am drawn to; it is only the author's clear sense of involvement and location within the poem that in the end draws me to poems. I believe that the most personal and intimate poetry is the poetry that can say the most: by focusing we actually allow the small-scale, the precious, to expand out into a shared readership. Another poet I admire, Mark Strand, uses a phrase which sums up what I am suggesting. He talks (in 'A Morning' from his *Selected Poems*) of "the one clear place given to us when we are alone".

John Burnside takes me to this "clear place", a place of focus, spirituality, preciousness and delight. His words contain some magic for me, evoke something important and timeless. What he writes about may be "common knowledge", but it is not a common gift to be able to write about it well. Now able to write about both dark and light, Burnside has the whole world to write about, and I look forward to further instalments of his work.

[*Acumen* 27, 1997]

A Notion of Sound

RUPERT LOYDELL INTERVIEWS DAVID TOOP

David Toop is a musician, composer, writer and sound curator. He has published three books: *Rap Attack* (now in its third edition), *Ocean of Sound*, and *Exotica* (selected as a winner of the 21st annual American Books Awards for 2000). His first album, *New and Rediscovered Musical Instruments*, was released on Brian Eno's Obscure label in 1975; since 1995 he has released five solo albums—*Screen Ceremonies*, *Pink Noir*, *Spirit World*, *Museum of Fruit* and *Hot Pants Idol*—and curated five CD compilations for Virgin Records—*Ocean of Sound*, *Crooning On Venus*, *Sugar & Poison*, *Booming On Pluto* and *Guitars On Mars*. *Needle in the Groove*, a collaborative album with novelist Jeff Noon, was released on Scanner's Sulphur label in May 2000

In 1998 he composed the soundtrack for *Acqua Matrix*, the outdoor spectacular that closed every night of Lisbon Expo '98 from May until September. He has recorded shamanistic ceremonies in Amazonas, worked with musicians including Brian Eno, John Zorn, Prince Far I, Jon Hassell, Derek Bailey, Talvin Singh, Evan Parker, Max Eastley, Scanner, Ivor Cutler, Bill Laswell and Haruomi Hosono, and collaborated with artists from many other disciplines, including theatre director/actor Steven Berkoff, Japanese Butoh dancer Mitsutaka Ishii and writer Jeff Noon. As a critic he has written for many publications, including *The Wire*, *The Face*, *The Times*, *The Sunday Times*, *The Observer*, *Arena*, *Vogue*, *Spin*, *GQ*, *Bookforum*, *Pulse*, *Urb* and *The Village Voice*. He curated *Sonic Boom*, an exhibition of sound art showing at the Hayward Gallery, London, from April to June, 2000.

Other projects currently in progress include the composition of a soundtrack for Mondophrenentic (*37th Floor At Sunset: Music For Mondophrenetic* CD to be released by Sub Rosa in August 2000), and a CD-ROM installation created in Belgium. In January 2000 he exhibited the sound installation *Dreaming of Inscription On Skin* with Max Eastley at ICC in Tokyo. He is currently a visiting Research Fellow at the London Media School.

I first met David Toop when he gave a reading from and fielded questions about *Ocean of Sound* as part of the Litmus: Spacex Literature and Music series of events I promoted in Exeter. Since then I have kept in sporadic e-mail contact. Visiting the *Sonic Boom* exhibition this spring prompted me to ask David for an interview. Sometime later, after visits to Japan [David] and the States [me] which have delayed things, here it is.

RUPERT LOYDELL: *Am I right in thinking this is a very "public" year for you? Your presence is manifest in the* Needle in the Groove *CD with Jeff Noon, with* Rap Attack 3, *and at the Hayward where you've curated* Sonic Boom.

DAVID TOOP: Yes, relatively public and very full. The last six years have felt like bursting out of a prison, letting go, just releasing material of all kinds. Creating a soundtrack for Expo in Lisbon two years ago was a big step for me. The daily audiences were so huge, the project took so long and working with that kind of multi-national team was a real eye opener. I know that at one time in my life I would have been almost phobic about that, quite terrified, but then I realised that those situations are full of potential, despite the problems that come with mass communications and big budgets.

Sonic Boom was an opportunity to put a certain personal view of sound and music across on a bigger scale, but also a chance to place artists and musicians I admire in the public earshot. More than 36,000 people visited *Sonic Boom* and aside from feeling proud of that, I'm interested to see what effect it has in the future. So having a public year has "career" implications, but it also cause certain effects that aren't possible when you're working, as I have done for most of my life, at the furthest possible distance from the centre of mainstream culture.

So how did you get here from there?—"there" being [I think I'm right] a member of the LMC in its draughty Camden upstairs room incarnation, with a commitment to the extreme fringes of improvisation; "here" being a respected musician, exhibition curator, compiler of CD anthologies, and respected and critically-revered writer on a variety of topics, from rap through An Ocean of Sound *to exotica and muzak.*

The London Musicians Collective wasn't year zero for me. When I was at art school in 1968 I was interested in putting on events and even before then, when I was at grammar school, I co-produced a little magazine, wrote music criticism (or at least plagiarised the sleeve-notes of blues albums I owned), put on art exhibitions and music/visual shows. The critical point for me was when I left art school. I was quite remote from any feeling of being in the "real world", playing intense improvised music with Paul Burwell and experiencing a strong sense of detachment from "the scene", even though we were sufficiently part of it to get reviews as "up and comers" from people like Martin Davidson and Ian Carr. We even did a

Jazz Workshop for Radio Three in 1973, though the BBC has either lost or erased the original tape.

Paul and I were collaborating with artists in different fields—sound poet Bob Cobbing, an amazing Butoh dancer called Mitsutaka Ishii, visual artists and performance artists like Carlyle Reedy and Marie Yates. There was a strong need to analyse all the time: what are we doing, why are we doing it, what is the significance of sound in our society, what did it or does it mean in other cultures? I felt cursed by that. I'd go out a lot, to places like the 100 Club to see Ray Russell or the Chris McGregor Group, and wish I could just enjoy it, the way the rest of audience seemed to be just giving themselves up to the music while I was sitting there, soaking up details, having opinions, reflecting. Tortured young man in front row!

I was also spending a lot of time with the Lathams, trying to understand what John Latham was talking about with his time base theory, usually failing but developing my own ideas as I listened. As well as getting a lot from the people I directly worked with, I was very influenced by John Stevens, who I seem to miss a lot, even though I couldn't say I was a close friend of his. Paul and I used to attend his workshops in Ealing, hosted by Christopher Small, who's now pretty well known for writing books on music. John was a great communicator, even though he could talk you into submission. He also had a knack of instilling confidence in novice musicians like me, and fostering an appreciation of improvisation as a complex craft, a touchstone you can come back to when you lose yourself or lose the direction of your music.

Most of my current ideas on writing and music formed at that time, 30 years ago. I was soaking up information and pouring out ideas but for various reasons, I didn't know how to get them across. I made radio programmes, for Radio Three, but three radio programmes in three years wasn't going to do much, particularly since nobody seemed to have a clue what they were about. Having that long gap of years between the imagining and the realisation has been frustrating and absolutely crucial. Twelve years in the sweat shops of mainstream journalism really taught me how communicate to at least some part of a mass audience. How to tell a story, in other words. At the same time, there's a lot of material stored up. If I'd been publishing books and records since the early Seventies I'd probably be knackered.

You put a new twist on some of the Virgin anthologies you compiled by introducing them with fiction, short stories, something that presumably links to both the new CD with Jeff Noon and the Buried Dreams *CD some time back with Max Eastley. Did you just get bored with writing standard-issue sleeve notes?*

Did I? I used to write press biographies for pop stars. I got so fucked off with it that I'd demand more money than I thought they'd pay, then say I'd only do it as a short story. It really started with *Buried Dreams*, though. We wanted the album to be more than just a bit of plastic with a music carrier inside. I was interested in the idea of writing short stories as a score for the music, like storyboards for a film, so the stories ended up on the sleeve-notes, then found their way into *Exotica*, then became the basis of the *Hot Pants Idol* CD I did. I like to remix what I do all the time.

The point about the compilations was that I felt compilations tend to ruthlessly narrow the focus of musical listening. Invariably, they concentrate on one genre or style, then package the collection within a strong aesthetic, with particular styles of contextualisation framing the idea of how listening should happen. That's as true of a brilliantly packaged archival box set as it is of some TV advertised Greatest Love Songs package.

Listening with any kind of freedom becomes almost impossible. I didn't want explanatory notes, either explaining my choices or filling in the history of the music, and Simon Hopkins, who was responsible for that series, totally backed me up. I wanted people to hear a segue from George Clinton into Michael Prime and sort it out for themselves. So the notes were a joke. One reviewer—otherwise very positive about what I do—described them as terrible, sub-Burroughs science fiction. That was amusing, because they were deliberate and affectionate parodies of cyberpunk, the Burroughs of *Nova Express*, crime fiction, Joseph Conrad, and so on.

The notes for *Sugar and Poison*, for instance, were a parody of Jack Womack's extraordinary grammatical perversion of the language, which I was knocked out by. With that particular compilation, I was sick and tired of the way soul ballads had been dismissed as romantic escapist drivel over the years by intellectuals of all persuasions and colours and then ended up being packaged by record companies as generic fuck soundtracks. The relationship between the notes, the artwork and the music was an attempt to create unease, to make a gentle push towards listening at a depth beneath the preconceptions about what was being said in the lyrics, the vocal techniques, the tempo, the type of chords, the arrangements and all the other indicators of genre stereotypes. I suppose some people thought it was a fuck soundtrack for manic depressives. Personally, I find that album overpoweringly romantic, even though it's supposed to be a bit disturbing, but then romance is disturbing in itself.

Jeff Noon's Needle in the Groove *book is full of dub and chrome, city streets and flickering lights, techno and dance music. Your CD project of the same name doesn't seem to reflect the hard-edged dance music of the book; how did you decide to ignore all that, along with the book's theme of remixology, and go for a more ambient, exploratory approach?*

It's almost impossible to read in a flexible, expressive way over hard-edged dance music. That's one practical issue that I was aware of, having tried it, so I didn't want to subject Jeff to the same difficulties. Second thing is, I heard something other than dance music in the book. I heard a weird soup of skiffle, blues, hip-hop beats, Manchester rock and psychological noise (if that doesn't sound too pretentious).

The remixing in the book is some new form of remix, a technology that we don't have and that doesn't bear much resemblance to the likes of Fatboy Slim, so I took a huge collection of fragments and jammed them all together in the computer. I was trying to make a total scenario—the physical environment of the book, the emotional and psychological landscapes, some sense of this musical confusion and interpersonal turmoil—and then give it a depth that you could fall into the way the characters fell back into their own past.

Many of your recent CDs have been collaborative projects [although I understand some of that is you mixing together recorded offerings from around the world]. Could you share some favourite moments in the making of your music, or of the interaction—musical or otherwise!—that produces your music?

I work really quickly and don't mess about. I don't take drugs. I don't drink alcohol when I'm making music. I eat fruit and drink water. I'm really boring. Because of that, and because of who they are, musicians come in and work in a really focussed way. I can't stand all that hanging around in studios, prevaricating and talking about nothing.

On *Pink Noir*, Talvin Singh heard the track for the first time in the studio, set up his tablas, conceived an interlocking part in his head and then played it by overdubbing himself just once. The two parts fitted together perfectly. He's a great musician. Evan Parker played without having heard the track and tore it up. I try to play everything in one take, just to instill some feeling of instantaneity or spontaneity or "danger" into electronic music, and everybody I work with seems to do the same.

One thing I found really funny when I recorded *Screen Ceremonies*, back in 1995, was the fact that the engineer knew why I wanted to use a bucket of water. He knew I was going to play flutes in it, even though he didn't know anything about me. That's progress. Now I record at home and I don't have to think about the cost so much, or have to justify doing ridiculous things to an engineer who thinks it's daft or argues that it won't work. But I really enjoy working with artists like Max Eastley because they bring extraordinary ways of working to mundane environments. I wanted to record Max's Violet Ray Vitalator, a crackling glass tube that you pass over your skin. He has a couple of these things that he inherited from his father, who was an avid, or more than avid collector. The Vitalator was a peculiar device that was supposed to give energy and cure medical complaints with electricity—a sort of early 20th century aromatherapy. Of course, it made a fucking huge electrical hum so you move very quickly from the absurdity of the situation to the technical challenges that have to be solved. That allows everybody to relax, particularly the engineer, and then the sound becomes the focal point of the session, rather than the eccentric means or technology used to produce it.

How do you feel about the time it has taken for people like yourself and Brian Eno to be accepted seriously by the music industry [or part of the music industry]?

Brian was accepted a long time ago, because of Roxy Music. I don't have a Roxy Music in my back pages; just the Flying Lizards, which doesn't have quite the same credibility. A student asked me the same question recently and wondered if it made me cynical. Being cynical about these things is corrosive. If it's true what you say about acceptance, and I'm not sure I believe it, then I'm glad it's happening for me now, at the age of 51, rather than having it happen to me at 21 and now be a fucked up old git with nothing left to say. But what I'm proposing in my writing is something different and whether that view of music turns out to be useful or not, the fact that it doesn't fit with received opinions about music means there's going to be a long delay before it begins to filter through to a slightly wider audience. That's how you'd want it, surely. Otherwise it's just a shiny new version of what's gone before. As for the music industry, I don't feel part of it, though I accept I have connections with aspects of it.

How do you personally navigate through all the music around these days? Ocean of Sound obviously offered one idea of making links and manoeuvring through genres, countries and time; more and more of us seem to have had to adopt ideas of networks and webs as a tool for exploration [maybe even survival when overload kicks in...].

I listen to music these days because I'm drawn to it for some reason. Maybe it becomes relevant to what I'm feeling or maybe somebody gave me a CD and I'm curious to hear what the person who gave it to me sounds like. Going to Japan, I'm given loads of CDs and working through them, trying to work out where they fit, is quite absorbing. I've just been asked to write a review of an Astor Piazzolla biography so I pulled all my Piazzolla records off the shelves and started listening as I read. It's like falling in love all over again but I'm hearing what's in the grooves in the light of the experiences I've had since I first discovered his music.

To be honest, I don't listen to that much music by other people these days. I spend a lot of time on my own music and when I'm writing, I can't concentrate if I listen. I live in a house with a partner who likes The Eels and a daughter who likes Britney Spears, so my listening time is limited anyway. I may not love their musical tastes but I love them so it helps me to become more tolerant. I also like to concentrate on one or two albums. For years I flitted about from album to album, track to track. I had to. I was being sent every new release and was expected to know the entire sweep of musical activity and be able to write about it all. Recently I've been listening a lot to a Japanese composer—Minoru Miki. I listened to him a lot in the mid-1970s and I've come back to him. I don't care he's not part of the fashionable canon. I listen to Sorabji as well, who is an oddity of 20th century composition, and pieces like Takemitsu's music for films like *Yotsuya Kaidan*. They have endless depths. I can catch up on new releases when I feel I'm genuinely interested to do so. I met Christophe Charles and Carsten Nicolai early this year in Tokyo—I liked them as people and I like what they're creating. Even though I've been listening to digital composers like them for some years, I'm only now getting a more complete picture of my own response to the changes that are taking place in music.

At the moment, I'm more excited to see the new Wong Kar-Wai film than any CD that's on the release schedule. Not that cinema is particularly dynamic right now, but there comes a point where you've heard so much.

David Toop

I realise I've been speed reading, or speed listening, for the past 16 years, ever since I became a professional writer. Now I've got shot of journalism, I can slow down again and listen with more thoroughness. I'd rather spend time cooking and studying food, which is more central to my life anyway, than keeping up with a million CDs.

Sonic Boom was obviously a major event; I'd like to move on to that now. If you don't mind, I'd like to start with what I perceived as some of the problems with the show. The first was the architecture of the show. I got very bored with peering into darkened rooms, and thought the gallery wasn't actually put to good use in many ways—there was a lot of empty space and shadowed corners in the Hayward. Did you consider putting more work in? Or asking the artists to make a different sort of work that considered the gallery space itself?

My original wish list of artists was much longer and I was persuaded to cut it right back. I learned the sense of that when the problems of budget restrictions, dealing with artist's demands, articulating space and administering other practicalities became evident. Now I feel the number was just about right. A lot of artists wanted to build rooms for themselves and I had a premonition of it becoming an exhibition of Portakabins. I understand that everybody want to isolate their work but certain artist really benefited from being brought out into the open. On the other hand, those dark rooms were absolutely essential. Clubs and concert halls are dark rooms. Shadows are a prerequisite for a large proportion of music.

Several of the pieces were very interesting, musically, but didn't seem to me very interesting visually—it was difficult, for instance, to find the Greyworld corridor installation visually stimulating; yet sonically it was one of my favourite pieces; Christina Kubisch's headphone installation likewise—visually it looked like the washing line spaces behind blocks of flats… Did you curate with the visual side given equal consideration?

My first priority was sound, but the brief was to make an exhibition that was also visually sophisticated. That's not easy, since works that are both visually and sonically exciting are quite rare. But I think there's more to it than a piece being visually striking. The Christina Kubisch, for example, was one of the most popular works in the show. I think that was partly because people had no expectations of it. They walked out onto the sculpture court with their headphones, found not much there other than lines of cable, put the headphones on and found themselves in a different world. The grin factor on that piece was very big.

I'm a bit puzzled by what you describe as the Greyworld corridor installation. Their work was outside, on the steps and the ramp leading to and from the Hayward. The only artist who had a corridor was Ryoji Ikeda. Ryoji wanted his ramped corridor to be sealed so that you experienced a total enclosure of whiteness, intense light and intense high frequency. The problem is that the gallery needs to have wheelchair access and with thousands of people tramping through, the carpet gets filthy. When you come to a gallery as a visitor you don't want to know about all these difficulties. You just want the perfect experience. But when you work at the sharp end, as a curator or organiser, then you have to make the best you can out of a lot of irritating obstacles to perfection.

I had no problem with the overspill of sound between pieces that some critics and reviews have mentioned, but it did seem to me some of the quieter pieces suffered in contrast to the "big" names and "big" installations. Max Eastley's sculptures were wonderful, so was Lee Ranaldo's guitar with it's little projection inside; but both were difficult to find within the show—I mean "psychically" [perhaps?] rather than physically: they didn't necessarily make their presence known to the exhibition visitor.

You had to find them, you had to work to find them. I wanted Max to have a lot of pieces in the show because his work is so quiet and undemonstrative. You'd turn a corner and find another piece by Max and my hope was that eventually the point would emerge through accumulation. One day I saw a whole line of people listening to Max's biggest installation—*Procession of Ghosts*—all of them in a line with their ears really close to the dancing wires. The issue of overspill is very subjective. Ultimately, it represented my idea of a sound exhibition, in which sound spill was a strong element within the perception of the show as a whole. Some critics wrote about the overspill as if it was an issue I wasn't aware of, or hadn't thought through.

And, playing devil's advocate [and pretending not to have read the subtitle "art of sound"—as opposed to music], how would you answer the retort that this sonic exploration is all well and good, but it isn't, in itself, music? I'd like to ask quite seriously, too, what you think about the idea that much improvisation should be regarded as research, and needs applying, filtering back into the mix as it were?—much as scratched beats are now an everyday occurrence in pop/chart songs.

I despise this functional approach to music. As I said in my first answer, improvisation is a craft that can occupy a lifetime. It can be applied in all musical situations but it's not a fucking effect that you stick into something more important or more "finished". The distinctions between music, sound and noise are ongoing and fluid and contextual and subjective. To me, that's not the problem. The difficulty lies in developing qualitative and usable evaluations of the thing we call music. Why is one piece great and another piece rubbish? Otherwise it's all just a tidal wave of stuff.

When noise, or sound, does work in a simple way on its own it still generates an emotional and physical thrill/response, sometimes in a way I thought I'd left behind as I reached my 40th birthday! I'm thinking specifically of the wonderful, unholy racket of the dragged guitar in Christian Marclay's exhibit. Any comments on that? You're obviously someone who still responds to all sorts of music—does that include revelling in noise itself?

One of my current side projects is archiving the many hours of tape made by the Alterations quartet of Peter Cusack, Terry Day, Steve Beresford and myself. There are companies wanting to release some CDs but hours of live recordings need to be monitored, transferred into the computer, edited, then transferred to CD. What surprises me is how much I'm enjoying the racket we made. A lot of unabashed noise, sometimes really childish and vulgar and sometimes very controlled and quite gorgeous (I can be that flattering about a band I was in because it was so long ago it feels fairly detached).

What also surprises me is that you make a connection in your question between growing older and losing an engagement with the sensuality of sound. I find it's the opposite. As I grow older, the distinctions between categories—noise, sound, music, silence—become genuinely less meaningful. In other words, it's no longer something I'm reading about in John Cage and then trying to apply.

I mentioned food and cooking earlier. That structural distinction that Lévi-Strauss wrote about in books like *The Raw and The Cooked* is still very interesting. Is noise raw food and music cooking? Mmmm, not quite but... a lot of Japanese cooking may seem to be just food—sushi, for example, a seaweed salad, or tofu in iced water—but in fact it's a remarkably artful form of cooking that blurs the distinction between nature and culture. That's also true of Japanese gardening. The way a tree is trained creates an impression of age and weathering. Quite artificial, in fact.

In theory, the more mature you get, the more you should be able to appreciate qualities such as astringency, bitterness and sharpness. When I came to Exeter to read for the event you organised a few years ago, I remember David Sawyer, the instrument inventor, talking to me afterwards about children and their eating habits. He claimed that children have more sensitive palettes than adults. I think that's true from observing the changing diet of my own daughter and cooking for her. Now she's 10 she's able to eat some Thai food, soba noodles or South Indian food and finding it more interesting than chicken nuggets and all the other bland frozen stuff that small kids love.

But unmediated noise is just a beautifully rich conglomeration of tones. The fact that it's raw, rather than cooked, means that we can be absorbed by tonal relationships and rhythms that are quite alien to human motivation. Their apparent randomness conforms more to general scientific principles than human characteristics and we can learn from that. That distinction— nature and culture—is one of the formulations that has always fascinated me and one of the defining aspects of digital music is that it hovers on the edge between human decisions and machine processes. A lot of it is music that grows within a software environment. A kind of digital moss. That's something we all have to get used to.

[*Tangents*, 2000]

David Toop

Shifting Patterns

AN INTERVIEW WITH NICHOLAS ROYLE

Nicholas Royle is the author of four novels—*Counterparts, Saxophone Dreams, The Matter of the Heart* and *The Director's Cut*—and more than a hundred short stories, as well as being the editor of ten anthologies. This interview came about as the result of Nicholas Royle contacting me having read my review of *The Director's Cut* at *Tangents* online. I'm grateful to Nicholas Royle for his time and interest.

RUPERT LOYDELL: *Your books are full of shifting patterns and themes, layers of meaning, that the reader has to order for themselves: is this a fair comment?*

NICHOLAS ROYLE: Yes, it's fair comment. Although there's plot and structure and narrative drive—at least I hope there is—the material is,to some extent, organised around echoes of certain images and obsessions. Layers of meaning is right as well. Not only do I not mind if some readers don't pick up on everything, but there's often stuff I don't expect anyone but the sharpest reader to get. It keeps it more interesting for me that way, and, I like to think, for the reader. This is not to say that my books are intended to be difficult to read. I want them to be read and understood without difficulty. At the same time, I accept they'll never sell like Jeffrey Archer's.

Is it impossible in the 21st century to write unambiguous novels? For the author to be omnipotent, the story to resolve? Or is the world as you see it too fragmented and chaotic?

I can't write unambiguous novels. I couldn't in the 20th century and I can't in this. A certain level of ambiguity is fundamental to all my writing, just as it is to life. Take the ambiguity away and I'd have very little interest in carrying on writing.

You are very concerned with place in your novels, particularly decaying Europe in Saxophone Dreams *and West London in* The Director's Cut. *How do you feel about the kind of detail you use to conjure up these places? Do you run a risk of alienating those readers who don't know the place? I mean I loved all the Shepherd's Bush and White City detail, as I grew up in the area, but others will not have the map in their head that I do, and will not be able to trace the novel's landscape in quite the same way.*

I've always liked fiction that deals with place quite specifically. I enjoy writing it, too. At the same time, I like stuff that's set in entirely invented places, such as Rupert Thomson's *The Insult*, to name just one recent example. I can't afford to worry about those readers who will switch off if I name too many actual streets or describe existing buildings. If they don't get it, they don't get. Too bad. For them and for me.

In The Matter of the Heart *you concern yourself with place in a different way, where a single powerful action occurring in a room resonates throughout history, affecting everything else that happens in that location—even when the room's use is changed, or the building that contains it is redeveloped. The power of the site and the action remains. Writers like Iain Sinclair and Peter Ackroyd have also played with this theme—do you share their belief in the occult power of place, or is it just a literary device?*

I am so strongly drawn to the idea I think I must believe it. If I weren't a writer, I would still have this same fascination with buildings. It's a part of my character, perhaps my nature. I do think that certain buildings have presence, or presences. And not just buildings either: knock a building down and it's hard not to believe that some sense of it persists. Perhaps in the way that we maintain that the dead remain alive as long as they rest in our hearts.

The Director's Cut *concerns itself with "re-inventing the self": characters assume identities, create and become new characters, take on other people's projects and names; film is also involved, making us think about how real life and celluloid life intermingle. This flux seems to fascinate you, yes? Is it another type of ambiguity?*

I've always been interested in questions of identity, and I've always been interested in film. This novel is the first time I've really fused those two interests.

You have championed the books of Steve Erickson in this country, a writer who writes strange surrealistic novels, where time slips and fragments slowly drift together into some semblance of a story; which changes again when one reads another book of his, as his whole output seems to be one long novel. Can you say what fascinates you about his work so much? And any other authors who have been important to you—either as influence or just as a good read.

Erickson is a genius. His imagination constantly amazes and thrills me. It also amazes me that he's so little known when other writers doing not dissimilar stuff are fêted to high heaven. The problem, in the UK at least, has been that he's been shunted from one publisher to another. None of them has put any real money into pushing his work. His first book, *Days Between Stations*, was a B-format paperback original—it hardly said prestige. It's a fact of the business that you need to dress something up in all the finery—hardback, big marketing spend, blah blah blah, if you want it to stand a chance of succeeding on any level. As you say, there's a story arc in his work that continues from on book to the next. He's creating a whole world and he does so with such flair and brilliance that you go with him. Other writers who've influenced me include M John Harrison, Iain Sinclair, JG Ballard, Derek Marlowe, Alain Robbe-Grillet, Roland Topor, Kafka, Christopher Burns. I could go on. There are so many.

You work at Time Out *magazine; I used to edit* Event South West, *a similar listings magazine for Devon, Somerset & Cornwall. I wondered if you feel, as I felt at the time, that apparently being on top of—or at least aware of—everything that happens, from gigs and club events through to endless new music and book releases, that time does work differently. I learnt to distance myself from a lot of this information, but even so there were always piles of review books around I wanted to read, LPs that I wanted to hear, concerts and events I wanted to attend. You may, of course, simply be able to distance yourself from it all, or be more organised or less susceptible! I guess I'm trying to talk about the idea of the "transitory" here, and about media overload.*

It's true that I'm sent a lot of books and I end up reading a lot of them, too many really, because I have very little time for my own stuff. I no longer review a book a fortnight, as I did at one time, whether I liked the stuff or not, because life is too short. I got really sick of reviewing any old rubbish. Now I'll just do something I really really care about, especially if no one else is going to do it. Luckily I don't get asked to do music, although I'm always buying new music, which I listen to when I'm working. I watch films constantly as well. I'm always slipping a few reviews of things we've missed into the *Time Out Film Guide*. I wouldn't say I'm on top of the arts scene in London, however; it's far too broad and diverse for that.

When you first contacted me, you were intrigued that I'd mentioned "symbolism" in a review of your last book. I backed down on that one, said it was probably the wrong word to use, but I wondered if you do ever use symbolism? I know you are interested in surrealism, and surrealism does, or did, come hand-in-hand with lots of heavyweight theories about dreams and sexuality and the mind's workings.

I've never consciously used symbolism. I eschew dream interpretation and use of the word "Freudian". I think that it's possible to have a tall thin building in a landscape without its necessarily being a phallic symbol. People who reduce everything to phallic this and vaginal that bore the arse off me, to be honest. I love surrealism and have done since I was able to appreciate art at any level. I like it in writing and film, but primarily in visual art.

We've also touched upon music in our initial correspondence prior to this interview. I suggested that the best books "about music" often aren't about music itself, but about what happens around music—either literally or metaphorically. I don't find musicians particularly interesting characters in real life or fiction: it's the music that is interesting. Saxophone Dreams both indirectly and directly concerns itself with jazz. Can you talk a little about that? Jazz has always been perceived as a more revolutionary music in Eastern Europe than it has in the West. What else do you listen to? Does it inform the way you make and pattern your books?

I listen to lots of jazz, as well as all sorts of electronic/ambient music, while I'm working. It cuts out other distractions and helps me work. Something that either meanders along in the background or chugs along energetically works just as well. I love the freedom of jazz, although I don't have much time for free jazz, if that makes sense. I like just about everything on ECM and all sorts of other jazz, too, mainly instrumental, as vocals distract if I'm working. Plus I listen to Scanner, JBK (Steve Jansen, Richard Barbieri, Mick Karn), Harold Budd, Jah Wobble, Brian Eno and lots of others. I find it difficult to address the subject of why music's so important to me. It just is. I mean, you just have to listen to it to see why.

You briefly ran a small press; your stories continue to appear in small magazines. Is this where talent is nurtured and found, as we editors like to think? What do you make of the way the book trade is changing, of the apparent fragmentation of readership and publishing itself?

Talent is discovered and nurtured in the small press, but an awful lot of crap is published as well. But that's the same as the mainstream publishers. Most of what comes out is instantly recyclable. Magazines such as *The Third Alternative, Ambit, Crimewave* and others continue to publish good stuff by new writers. I try to publish new writers myself in the anthologies I do for *Time Out*, although there's not so much enthusiasm at the moment for doing those anthologies. Short stories don't sell, they're always telling us. It may be true that they sell less well than novels, but that's not the point. The point is short stories are a valid form and there will always be an audience for them, whatever its size.

Can you tell us what else you are working on at the moment, and when your next novel is due?

A sequel to *The Director's Cut* called *Straight to Video*. It's set in Antwerp and I'm about a quarter of the way into it. It won't appear before spring 2002 at the very earliest. Probably the autumn, considering the rate at which it's progressing.

[*Stride*, 2001]

Something Dynamic

AN INTERVIEW WITH ANDREW POPPY

As a teenager Andrew Poppy experimented with *musique concrète*, played Beethoven on the piano and bass guitar in an improvising rock band before going on to study music at Goldsmith's College.

During his time at Goldsmiths he was active as a performer organising performances of Terry Riley's *In C* and other experimental works, as well as playing the piano in Webern's *Concerto* and giving a solo piano performance of Glass's *Music in Fifths*. His interest in an alternative contemporary music was especially stimulated by contact with American composers Christian Wolff and John Cage. On graduating in 1979 Poppy worked as an accompanist at The Laban Centre of Dance and Movement giving him an education into the world of contemporary dance.

In early 1981 Poppy became a founder member and pianist with The Lost Jockey, a large ensemble which explored in both composition and performance the pulse based techniques associated with the work of Glass, Reich and Andriessen. He wrote a number of works for the ensemble including, The Object is a Hungry Wolf.

Poppy's attempt to recontextualise this music and gain access to a wider audience came in the mid 1980s when he signed as a recording artist to Paul Morley and Trevor Horn's ZTT Records. Enthusiastically pursuing a post minimal aesthetic in the context of a pop label he recorded 2 CDs. The first, *The Beating of Wings* contains 3 fully notated works (including 32 Frames for Orchestra) and Listening In, a type of studio work further developed in his second CD *Alphabed*. This album clearly merges traditional composition and studio production techniques in its use of sequencers, samples and electronic keyboards and includes a variety of singers including Annette Peacock, Ashley Slater, Udo Scheuerpflug and Dee Lewis. Two 12-inch releases show the extent to which Poppy could use the studio to build new works out of the multi-track recordings of finished pieces. *The Impossible Net* remodels *32 Frames* whilst *Kink Konk Presto, Kink Konk Adagio, East Fragment* reinvents *Listening In*.

During the 1980 Poppy collaborated on experimental/visual theatre pieces produced by The Institute of Contemporary Art in London such as Secret Gardens and Midday Sun. This interest developed into a number of music theatre or chamber opera works: *The Songs of the Claypeople* for Impact Theatre and *The Uranium Miners Radio Orchestra Play Scenes From Salome's Revenge* for Royal Opera House's Garden Venture. In 1991 The National Theatre Studio commissioned *Baby Doll* a chamber opera for 3 voices, adapted from a Tennessee Williams' screen play and in 1996 the composer wrote and recorded *Ophelia/ Ophelia* an opera and version of *Hamlet* for one voice which was selected by the

International Society for Contemporary Music to be part of the year of culture festival in Copenhagen.

In the 1990s a renewed interest in concert music produced *14 Poems and Toccatas for violin and piano*, (performed at the Huddersfield Festival by Andrew Ball and Elizabeth Perry) and Ember: String Quartet for The Balanescu Quartet. *Eight Movements for Piano Trio, Eleven Word Title, Sprung and Suspended* and *End Synch Sound* (with a film) were commissioned by various chamber ensembles. In 1997 the Royal Liverpool Philharmonic Orchestra commissioned Horn Horn a concerto for 2 alto saxophones and orchestra. Most recently New York pianist Jed Distler and UK based Tania Chen have performed selections from Fruits and *Shavings*, 23 pieces for solo piano.

Over the last two decades Poppy has contributed to the creative projects of many other artists. This includes working in the studio with bands such as The The, Erasure, Nitzer Ebb as well as making theatre scores for Julia Bardsley's productions of *Macbeth* and *Family Reunion* and Kenneth Branagh's performance of *Coriolanus*. The list of choreographies provoked to make dances to Poppy's music include Ian Spink, Sally Owen, Michael Clark, Gaby Agis, Sue Davies, Linda Gaudreau, Julia Bardsley, Michael Popper, David Massingham and most recently New Yorker Heidi Latsky. He has also made music for TV and film— notably with Portuguese director and producer Vitor Gonçalves—and between 1995-97 he was head of music at the National Film and TV School in the UK.

The year 2000 saw the CD release of *Time At Rest Devouring Its Secret*, a studio work of 35 minutes duration which once again connects the musical techniques of the minimalist project to an image from popular culture.

§

RUPERT LOYDELL: Your new CD, *Time At Rest Devouring Its Secret*, seems to have be very much of the moment, in that it shows affinities to both the quiet-sounding and -paced music of Morton Feldman and Takemitsu, and to early electronic music. These musics are very fashionable at the moment: there's been a flurry of releases and re-releases by the former, and compilations like *Ohm*: the early gurus of electronic music and Early Modulations anthologising the latter. Is this just fortuitous or are you very aware of trends and movements in contemporary music? I ask this partly because at the time of your first album, *The Beating of Wings*, there were groups like Lost Jockey and Regular Music drawing on the then fashionable hybrid of minimalism and rock dynamics.

ANDREW POPPY: I hope to keep aware of what is going on and I think I've done my own share of moving things along, changing things.

I've always been interested in electronic music and the recording process since I was at school in the 60s when I discovered Stockhausen's *Kurzwellen* and Pierre Henry's *The Door and the Sigh* piece. They were inspirational along with all the psychedelic multi-track stuff that the Beatles did in the studio. Tape as a material and process was an extraordinary inspiration then and still is even now. I still work with analogue sometimes. Seeing what happens when you turn the tape over is always a revelation, a transformation! How much I'm a fashion victim is something for you have to decide.

The basic material and the idea of the process of *Time at Rest* was made around 1989 and I kept coming back to the work during the 1990s trying to find a way to make the piece. To find out what it might be about. It didn't really come into focus until late 1999. Perhaps it was that during the '90s I tried to re-engage with traditional performance with musicians again; to get away from the multi-track studio and the computer and make shorter piece. But recently I'm trying to integrate some of those ways of working having now made quite a lot of notated concert music. For instance there is a notated version of *Time at Rest* that works with the recording.

I was in both Regular Music and Lost Jockey at their beginning. I was particularly responsible, for what it is worth, for trying to position Lost Jockey in a more popular cultural context. The dusty musty academic world of new music concerts and competitions always really depressed me. It's like some old boys club. So I approached *Melody Maker* and John Gill at *Time Out* to do features about the Jockey. I pointed to the connections between Terry Riley and Kraftwerk in what we did. Both of whom at the time (1981) had some currency outside the academic music context. At the time Glass and Reich were still very esoteric, whereas Riley had the psychedelic "hit" of sorts with *A Rainbow in Curved Air* in 1971. My idea was not that we were doing pop music but that the music we were making could have a real audience. Not just one of music students. After I left Lost Jockey I continued to approach adventurous record labels with tapes rather than seek out a publisher with scores, which is the traditional route for a composer.

I think I'm right in saying Time At Rest *is very much a studio composition? You talk in the statement you sent me about the work in terms of duration, texture and performance. Can you elaborate this, perhaps sharing the process of composition [i.e. the intent and ideas behind the piece] as well as the process of making the music in the studio? I'm especially intrigued by your idea that "the part played by the mix is performance".*

What I mean by performance is something dynamic, fluid, spontaneous and unique at a particular moment in time. Unconscious and not rationally motivated. Something lived in the moment as opposed to the constructed and conceptual work that might be called composition. It's a difficult one because composition involves spontaneity and the flow of unique moments as well. And of course some ways and traditions of making music don't conceive of composition as a separate work. Western Classical music is very particular in the separation of composition and performance. Notation is central to this. But anyway with something like *Time at Rest*, because it is so systematic I feel the need to mess it up a little, to blur things or to make them breath in a different way. So as the mix proceeds you engage with the moment, in the emotional life of the piece, listening creatively to the movement of the piece and things start to happen that you didn't hear before. Just the simple re-balance of stereo can bring some detail to the surface. This shapes the work in a different way from the imperatives of mechanical structuring.

Time at Rest started with a simple melody which was originally improvised then divested of all rhythmic detail by giving every pitch a equal duration and space. Turning it into pulse. This was then analysed in a simple statistical way. The tune generates a number of chromatic lines. The idea was that the repetition of pitch within the original melody was itself a rhythmic structure. All the repeated pitches then because the points to articulate a chromatic line. This isn't important to know when listening but I think it is one of the things that holds it together. The process is just out of reach perceptually. This keeps the tension within what seems to be quite a static texture. I've always been interested in the way chromatic lines provide tension in a static environment. *32 Frames for Orchestra* is a good example.

Another aspect I'm interested in is what I think of as fictional space and real space. Fictional space as in artificial reverbs and the position of sounds in the stereo image. Left/right forward/back (wet/dry). To some extent all recordings are electronic music because they are recordings. They have gone the transformational way of recording technology and are projected via loud speakers. Somehow they become performance again in the real space of the playback. Every room being unique, every speaker position, every set of ears. So the fictional space (the reverbs and panning) interacts with the real space of playback with its positions and reverbs. So I've been presenting *Time at Rest* in installation and performance modes and it seems to work very well. Especially in traditional performance venues. I first presented it in a studio theatre at the National Review of

Live Art in February then in March at The Space in Isle of Dogs. and then for 14 continuous performances at the Tramway in Glasgow on 28 29 April

You've always had an interest in variations, haven't you? Several pieces on your two ZTT albums were remixed for 12-inch releases. Was this your decision or was it part of the 1980s remix culture. Obviously, Trevor Horn was instrumental in creating and sustaining this remix movement, although he never got his hands on your tapes did he? Would you consider someone else mixing your music?

The way I work with variation isn't always like the classical theme and variation. Although the inspiration for something like *32 Frames* was late Beethoven variation form. The *14 Poems and Toccatas* on the *Recordings* CD are more like Schumann variations. Aspects of an environment, a world, like 'Carnival' or an unspoken theme.

I suppose Re-mixes are variations in some way. Today remixing often becomes re-composition. I really liked the way that Trevor was pioneering the remix. The idea of making a completely new piece inside the body of an old one is not so new. Compositions manual from the 18th century suggest just that: write a new bass line for a old tune or visa versa. The 3rd movement of Berio's *Sinfonia* was a great inspiration for me as a student. He took a Mahler movement and then gradually substituted each moment with "samples" from other orchestral works. Although the samples are completely written into the score and then played by the orchestra. It's like a version of Cage's collage techniques with radios but from the platform of high culture. A prophetic piece in some ways. I've heard that Luciano was bemused by *Sinfonia's* success. And you can understand why. The way the technique of collage challenges the position and skill of the European composer.

John Leckie told me that the Jamaica record industry used to thrive on the remodelling of tracks. Partly to reuse the expensive 2 inch multitrack, the backing tracks made by session players would be passed from one singer to another to make new tracks. The old vocal getting wiped out each time.

There is another track on a compilation released by the same company who've released Time At Rest, *yes? How do you feel about the company you keep there? Are you interested in electronica and experimental dance musics? What music informs your current preoccupations? Is that different from the music you listen to for relaxation or pleasure?*

Andrew Poppy

Blind Fold is for solo electric piano and released on souRce research recordings as part of Ian MacKinnon's *Emre: dark matter* project. I like different contexts. Support is where you find it. Ian's label has been a much needed injection of confidence. There's not much support in the new music community for what I've been doing for 20 years. The SPMN trumpet that they are an open society promoting lots of types of music. The reality is something else

I'm very interested in electronica and experimental dance music. But I listen to loads of different stuff. Any particular year I'm obsessing about something. Continuous faves of the last couple of years are the Mad Professor remix of Massive Attack's *No Protection*. Radiohead. During the '90s Schnittke, Gubaidulina, Takemitsu, and Feldman have dominated a lot of my thought and I acknowledge their influence on my work.

I have a problem trying to approach the "work and pleasure" bit of your question. When I go out to a club I may dance to the most horrible things if they have the necessary groove and are played loud enough. That may or may not be a pleasure. In fact I've had some moments of musical epiphany on the dance floor to those funky house tracks. I played Schnittke's *Concerto for Piano and String Orchestra* to some students recently. I hadn't heard it for 5 or 6 years and I was completely awe struck.

Last year I did some work with Claudia Brücken (Propaganda). We met up again recently and did a set of covers for solo piano and voice. Just as a way of getting to know one another musically. We did a little low-profile gig and we're hoping to work together again soon

Alphabed remains one of my favourite albums. I found it second-hand shortly after a friend taped The Beating of Wings *for me and suggested I'd enjoy it. (I did). It seems to me to be different from your other releases in the way it slots into what, for want of a better phrases, I'd call "experimental rock songs"—I'm thinking of work by Annette Peacock (who appears on the album), Robert Wyatt, perhaps Laurie Anderson. Is that fair? I wondered firstly, why you'd moved away from that area of music, and, secondly, whether* The Songs of the Clay People—*which is noted as "a work in progress" on the album sleeve—was ever completed. I'd love to hear further instalments.*

I'm really pleased you like *Alphabed*. For me it's about two things. *45* is is like a homage to Robert Wilson and Philip Glass of the *Einstein on the Beach* period. Although I didn't make it in that spirit. It was part of a music theatre work called *Songs of the Clay People* which itself came out of a collage poem that I wrote and then developed into a theatre piece with Impact Theatre. The second thing is the studio. More than any other album this is about being in the studio and working with technology. Although all the tracks were written in outline. Much of the detail of *Goodbye Mr G* was developed in the studio. There is another 45 minutes of music from that show which hasn't been successfully recorded.

I moved away from this area of work because I didn't have access to a studio after 'ZTT the '80s version' came to an end. I couldn't get a deal to continue what I was doing. There was a ZTT backlash I think. Although Daniel Millar at Mute was interested (I made several arrangements for Erasure and Nitzer Ebb) it never developed into a deal unfortunately. No deal, no studio, it's hard to make records, especially if you've been used to working in great studios with engineers like Stuart Bruce, Bob Kraushar Dave Meagan. I was very disillusioned with attempting to position what I did in the popular arena. Too often dismissed by journalist who know nothing about the music. I still think *Beating of Wings* is a production with ambition and range unmatched by anything in that area at the time. Yet at the end of the '90s I had no support and no idea of how to continue. It was very easy to see how business can pick you up when you seem to have a lot to offer, try you out for a couple of years and then drop you. I went back to the drawing board literally, to the pencil and paper and to the piano and got connected up to the compositional things that had been let slip in the studio. I wanted to make pieces that would work directly with straight forward performance. So just a piano and a violin or a string quartet. No electronic technology. Nothing to plug in. Just the musician and the instrument.

Was the live performance of the Alphabed *music in Paris as exciting as it looks on the album sleeve?*

The feedback I got was very positive. Picture and review in *Blitz* at the time. The opening of the Science and Technology Park at La Villette was on *News at 10* and Gary Maughen, one of the Fairlight programmers, told me you could hear a snatch of *45*. It's good to be witnessed. The French President enjoyed it!

Dare I ask what actually happened when ZTT closed? They seemed to have everything going for them and then it all imploded until their recent resurrection!

Andrew Poppy

I don't really know myself exactly what happened to ZTT. When I signed Trevor reassured me that they were committed to a 5-album deal and to me being able to develop as an artist there. It's true I did learn an enormous amount. They let me produce my own records. The only artist on ZTT to do so. Being close to what Trevor and Steve Lipson were doing was fantastic. They showed me how they were working on the Grace Jones project with 2 digital machines. I looked though the *Two Tribes* multi-track with Stuart Bruce. So elegantly put together as a production. Like a Brian Wilson thing. And the Art of Noise were around. Gary Langan and Ann Dudley. I was a big AON fan. That's why I'd gone to ZTT in the first place. I just wanted to make records really.

Towards the end when I was hanging around all the time waiting for studio down time to finish *Alphabed* Jill (MD at ZTT) said she'd get me some production work. I really wanted to work with Billy Mackenzie. I felt he never got the arranger/producer he deserved. But nothing every happen. The whole ZTT label seemed to evaporated sometime in 1987. They had legal problems with Island Records who they were obligated to for manufacture and distribution. There was some nest fouling going on I think. There was the Dave (Stiff) Robinson factor. He came in as label manager for a while. Don't understand that one. Don't think Robbo and Paul Morley were on the same planet aesthetically and at a conceptual level Paul Morley was fundamentally important to spirit and identity of ZTT. There's a lot to inverted snobbery in popular culture in the UK at least. The anti intellectual British bull dog mentality rules OK. All this coincided with Frankie and Propaganda and AON going the way of all things: litigation. It was all a bit of a mess at the end. Although I didn't leave on bad terms. My contract lapsed.

You haven't been tempted to rejoin their artists' roster I presume? although they've re-released your two albums.

My two albums were released by ZTT/Warners during the 90s when ZTT were licensed to them. Since that changed, ZTT are now with Universal, my ZTT records are unavailable. I'd love to do something with the label again but perhaps they don't have the optimism and adventurous spirit of the 1980s. I met Paul Morley at a party last year and he said if he'd been running ZTT I'd be on my 17th album by now. So…

The thing is, I learned that there are more ways to hatch a chicken. I mean my early ambition and drive was to be a musician/composer and make records. I'd made records under my own name so even though I felt insecure and alone at the end of the 80s I had achieved something. Although it's curious. I wasn't really aware that people had bought the records all over the world and were really into the music. It took 10 years for that to filter back. The internet has been great. When I started my own production company I'd started to get feed back. From all over: USA, Europe, Russia.

So after ZTT, about 1988, I re-focused. Put making records as a low priority. People like Graham Fitkin and Lawrence Crane have been very supportive. When Graham was composer in residence at Liverpool Philharmonic he and Duncan Fraser commissioned *Horn Horn*—the piece for 2 solo saxophones and orchestra. Having the chance to write for full orchestra again was a high point of the 90s.

Since then it seems your own work—from where I stand anyway!—has mainly been in the classical world, although I'm aware you have written for theatre and dance, made music for TV and film, and worked in the studio with several rock bands. Am I right in imagining a small world of contemporary classical listeners and record labels in the same way there is an "indie-rock" and "electronics" scene, or do you feel part of something more general and wider? Can you talk about the function of your own Bitter & Twisted Records & Productions company within the marketplace, and its role in furthering and nurturing your music? Do you record your work and then try and place it with a record company, or do they commission recordings?

The music is for anyone who wants to listen. I don't feel particularly connected to any one thing. I wish I did sometimes.

Bitter and Twisted Records and Production was set up as an umbrella for recording and live projects. Originally I wanted to have a label and release music by other composers but it's hard to finance. The Recordings CD was my own money and released on my label Bitter and Twisted. Again a great learning process: understanding the complete label process, especially at the promotion and distribution level.

Yes I'm part of something wider than the classical music ghetto. But I'm part of that tradition in the way that I organise my musical resource rather than being in the club. As Glyn Perrin once said you can't throw 2000 years of notation out of the window overnight. Perhaps he meant that it has to be modified and dismantled, re model, bit by bit even if you have played in a rock band.

The last few releases have been BTRAP productions licensed to different labels and recently working with Ian Mackinnon at souRce

Andrew Poppy

research recording has been a wonderful development. Obviously I've worked in music production since Lost Jockey and before. All my recordings are produced by me. I feel that the music production is part of the composition. I'm very grateful to all the labels that have released my work. I realise that it is an act of faith on their part. It's very hard to do the whole process oneself with very limited financial resources.

How do you see the music business in a few years time? It seems it has to deal with MP3 and the net, fragmentation and smaller, more genre-specific, sales and copyright issues on top of all that. Robert Fripp (and he isn't alone) has made a stand against record companies taking copyright away from composers and musicians. Do you think we will see moves—though maybe not in Top-of-the-Pops land—towards musicians retaining more control of their musical output, licensing their music to record companies as and when required? Fripp and King Crimson, for instance, seem to have various levels of release: official bootlegs released by subscription, more generally available releases on their own label, and mainstream releases licensed to a major record company for international releases.

It's a catch 22. Business will not invest in promotion unless it see the potential for return. Challenging work is always going to be "perceived to be" a high risk. I believe that unchallenging work is also a high risk commercially because no one really knows what will be a hit tomorrow. But this idea doesn't worry the accountant. What is important is that the accountant "believes" that challenging work is a high risk. So we're stuffed.

It's not possible to record or perform something like *32 Frames* without large-scale subsidy or the support of a commercial enterprise. I don't have access to either. With hard work and determination it's easy to do small scale things all yourself. Is it possible to promote properly without a budget? The new story is that the internet works like a super word of mouth. That it is possible to disseminate work without any promotional budget at all. I'm not sure that a few exceptions become a rule.

Many of your works seem to have a quite literary source, or at least component. The lyrics on Alphabed *are certainly more "poetic" than normal lyrics, and* Ophelia/Ophelia *draws on Shakespeare's* Hamlet. *Do you come at music— or this music—through language rather than initially hearing it?*

There is a whole aspect to what I do that is about finding the other side of language. What is behind the mirror of language. The way text shapes things is hard to say. In a song, perhaps it is clear. But in *Ophelia/Ophelia* for instance, the text is often scrambled by the abstract musical processes. I like this. Language is such a strong force. It's great to find a way to pull it off centre. It's that question of music and meaning. Ophelia says "'tis in my memory locked and you yourself shall keep the key of it". The meaning seems clear. Why should we sing? Literature is important to me, especially poetry. And I've been re-reading Borges again.

How does this contract with the more chamber-type music on Recordings? This group of work seems more traditionally "classical" than your other music. Is this deliberate, am I reading it wrong, or just a careful choice of work for a particular moment or release?

The CD *Recordings* is more overtly classical and not just the compositions. It's recorded straight to stereo. Recorded and edited like the Arditti might record. Live performances in a space. *Rude Bloom* tries to make the point about different recording processes with two sets of trios. The piano trio was recorded straight to stereo (almost) the other is sequenced and overdubbed with keyboards, drum machine, trumpet and sax.

Do you enjoy collaborations? How much freedom are you given when orchestrating for a rock band in the studio? Or when working on experimental theatre or performance pieces? Presumably scoring for film and theatre means you see the finished, or almost finished performance and work to that? Do you find that restrictive? How do you teach this way of making music?—you were head of music at the National Film & TV School in London for several years.

Almost all the orchestration I've done for bands I've been given a free hand. So I'm a collaborator in a way and I really enjoy this challenge. I try to work on projects where I feel that people want what I have to offer.

I love collaborating on hybrid forms that use music: theatre, dance, film. Although different artists are coming together to make a single work that single work is like a trick or convention of form. Dance and film and some types of theatre are hybrid and heterogeneous works. There is a book that I'm working on intermittently about this whole area of work and ideas.

There are as many approaches as people and productions. Also there is always more than one solution to any particular screen moment.

Running courses it's fascinating to give 10 composers the same film and see the responses. Of course some people make things that are wildly inappropriate. There are always a couple of great takes on the scene. The obvious solutions are usually the ones that work least well. It's not that every solution is right but that there is more than one appropriate solution to the sonic experience of any screen moment. Some people look at the picture too much I think. The successful score is one that creates space between the image and the sounds

The other thing is that the work isn't finished until the end of the process. We are all making it up as we go along. Just because there is a script, or a rough cut, doesn't mean the solutions are a foregone conclusion in the director or producers head. The two sides to the Hitchcock myth are 1) that he saw everything in his head before principal photography. Great. Preparation is essential part of any process; 2) He told Hermann not to score the shower scene in *Psycho*. Hermann ignored him because he had a different creative impulse. What do we have of the film today?

Your website lists two new projects you are working on: a collaborative "environment with moments of performance" and a new ensemble piece entitled Weighing the Measure or Why Pulse. *Can you tell me about these and any other new work?*

Avalanche Thoughts is the title of a collaborative work that Julia Bardsley and I are developing for a large gallery space in New York called "Gale Gates et al" in November 2001. The title comes from a set of piano pieces of the same name and the concept and material developed out of a short story by Ted Hughes into *Snow*, a short film by Julia. *Avalanche Thoughts* incorporates installation, performance, video projection, live and recorded music. Perhaps it will be a kind of Happening where everyone experiences being lost in the snow, for an hour and a half. We are hoping to bring it to UK next year if we can find a venue and a promoter.

Weighing the Measure is a work in progress estimated duration about a hour. Hopefully it's something to do with trance, dance and drone. It's something that I'm developing with a group of musicians in Rome. At the moment it's for drum machine patterns and ensemble but it's likely to change once the process gets under way.

[*Tangents* and *Stride*, 2001]

Shattered Preconceptions

Questions for David Kennedy

I always find it interesting how my preconceptions are so often shattered. I confess I had David Kennedy down simply as one of the editors of *The New Poetry*, a book I, along with many other writers, have always found curiously titled and notable mostly for the absence of the "new" within its pages. I had assumed that David Kennedy would be stuck in the curious timewarp of The New Poetry era, probably writing grim realist narrative poems.

How wrong I was! Last year I got my hands on a copy of Kennedy's *Cornell: A Circuition Around His Circumambulation*, a quirky mix of prose poetry, fragmentary essay and concrete poetry; and also The Fiery Chariot, an even stranger pamphlet exploring the world of alien abduction, with the mix this time including calligraphic work, illustrations, letters and poems. But it was the copy of *The President of Earth, a New and Selected Poems* [published by Salt] that really showed me how utterly wrong I'd been. Here were intelligent, accessible but syntactically slippery and quirkily written, poems I was sorry to have previously missed. Section 2 [of 3 sections in the book] especially intrigued me, and I read and re-read them before emailing David Kennedy about how he'd written that particular set of poems. After an initial email conversation I asked him if he'd be prepared to undertake answering some questions for Stride, a kind of email interview. The questions were sent to him early in October and the final answers emailed back in November.

§

RUPERT LOYDELL: *The President of Earth is subtitled "new and selected poems" but it doesn't read like a "traditional" selected, where the poet chooses 2 or 3 poems from early books, and then wodges from later books—it's much more organized as a book in its own right.*

DAVID KENNEDY: The book certainly does reflect a concern with shape and coherence. The "new and selected" merely reflects the fact that the poems date from the period 1987 to 2001. If I'd put in all the poems I'd ever written that I still thought were any good, the book would be very different. I didn't want to end up with a book that would have been akin to an album of snapshots. I wanted something that would be more interesting for the reader. And when I started to choose work, I realised that although plenty of the early poems still "stood up" they weren't really anything to do with me as either a poet or a person now. I do think that your relationship to poems—your own and others—is a renewable journey to somewhere that changes as and because you do. Once I'd started to reject and select poems in that way, then other themes seemed to emerge. One of those themes is the future. Anyone my age—early 40s—will have grown up with ideas that by the year 2000 we'd all be living in domes, traveling by monorail and not working because robots would be doing all that for us. Clearly, that hasn't happened—everyone seems to be working harder and longer than ever before and the government's talking about raising the retirement age to seventy. So I'm interested in exploring the lack of fit between what we were promised and what we've actually got, and particularly the way we still want to believe that the promise has come true. The title poem talks about that when the speaker says "This is the future I read about in school". 'Remembering the Future', which is a kind of oblique elegy for my father, engages not only with the past's ideas of the future but also with the way that, particularly in England, ideas of the future and the past are inextricably linked.

You've stated recently that despite using processes such as collage, you still wish your poems to be clear to the reader, particularly in the way they use language. Is this to do with style and vocabulary or are you still concerned with some kind of "message"? The first part of The President of Earth—*which are perhaps earlier poems?—might suggest this is the case. Indeed, some of the poems in the first part of the book are more "ordinary" as poems, with a punchline/ epiphanic ending.*

You're referring to the email exchange that preceded this interview. I think what I said was that I wanted to use plain language; but I meant that in the sense of unadorned not transparent. About half the poems in Part 1 date from the early to mid-1990s when I was interested in using poetry to think through cultural, social and political questions. I'm certainly not interested in messages but I am interested in responding to ideas, to things that are happening culturally, politically, etc; and I do want my readers to think. The poems in Part 1 are also a reaction against "I'm a poet—dig my lifestyle, feel my pain" anecdote poetry—e.g. here's a poem about our new house/new baby/last holiday/recent tragedy. I'm actually quite revolted by the ease with which a lot of poets write about their own lives and I also think it's a kind of substitute thinking in the sense that they're using apparently intimate facts about themselves to manipulate readers into feeling and thinking. I don't want my poetry to be a ready meal quick fix of carbohydrates made tasty with too much salt and sugar. That's why the poems about my late father—the three-part 'Father and Son' and 'Remembering the Future'—are quite oblique when compared with a lot of poems by sons about fathers. Or rather, I was more interested in exploring what it means to write poems of mourning and remembrance as opposed to just "doing" mourning and remembrance while being true to my own experience within that. When I was sitting by father's hospital bed as he lay dying, I did think that the blankets looked like all that peculiar matted stuff you used to see on the nose cones of space capsules; and when I was writing the poem many years later it occurred to me that death is a little like going off into space, into a cold void. But I didn't feel any need to say "Ooo look, it's just like…" I want to leave some work for the reader to do. It's what excites me as reader as well as being connected to my belief that the most important work in poetry generally is done by readers anyway.

To focus on the first part of *The President of Earth* specifically, it's called 'Histories' and that responds to a number of things. First, the ideas that have been around for a while—which I don't buy—that we're somehow at the end of something or have arrived at some kind of final destination. That's what is being mocked in the title poem as "the world's dream"; and is perhaps causing a little more anxiety in the two part 'Postmodern Scenes': "I miss the old stories, their creaky plots:/At least you knew where you were in the…" Second, and more, importantly, the fact that we're surrounded and bombarded with all sorts of stories that have pre-scripted roles for us. We buy into—maybe we're actively bought by—some of these stories without even realising it; and because the stories have to work through their various stages, our world changes and we're changed too. The hardest thing to do, in art and in life, is first to understand that we live inside change and then to step outside change and see it happening, understand its effects. This is one of the things that poetry is uniquely placed to do. It's partly what I'm getting at in 'A Walking Lunch' when the narrator wonders whether he's a "causeless effect" that perhaps not even "a double reading" can explain. It surprises me that you find some the endings work like punchlines or epiphanies. That rather assumes that the "I" in the poems is the same person as the David Kennedy you're interviewing—which certainly isn't the case. Thinking about the poems in those terms makes the apparent epiphanies and punchlines a lot less definite and more open to question.

Part 2, 'Cities', is a very lyrical series of poems that clearly relate to each other in some way (lines re-appear from other poems throughout the section; they all have the same shape on the page) and yet resist traditional interpretation

David Kennedy

*as a sequence of poems and indeed, sometimes resist any obvious "meaning";
yet they are playful and lyrical. Can you tell me about this group of poems?*

It interests me that you focus on the lyrical elements. The poems have
been called surreal and compared to Adrian Mitchell, which doesn't really
catch what they're about. I think the lyrical material that is present would
probably seem excessive in a more conventional context but seems to work
in poems that are generally excessive anyway and constantly swinging
from one mood to another. One thing I've been trying to think through
critically recently is the idea that poetry is concerned with different types
of excess. For example, it's often a form of play-in-language that wouldn't
be permissible in other contexts. Similarly, it's a place where all sorts of
things can be expressed that are otherwise unwanted or culturally homeless.
I discuss this in more detail in the essay 'Reading The Reading: Poetry as
Loss, Excess & Speaking With Dead' in the *Words Out Loud* volume that
Mark Robinson recently edited for you.

The poems in 'Cities' are all I wanted to collect from a sequence of 50
16 line "free sonnets", as I like to call them. The poems were written in an
intense burst between February and April 1993 and revised a little later
that year. I was looking at the original ms. when I was choosing poems for
The President of Earth and it surprised me how many seemed to be a case of
"first thought best thought" which is usually something I'd distrust if not
entirely reject. I started with a set of 20 which were collaged from several
old notebooks full of stuff that I'd never found the right home for. What
happened during the writing of the first 20 was that I started to use the
last line of one poem as the first line of another. After a while, I just carried
on free-writing and the collaging started to become using anything that
was happening as I was writing. And using the last line of one poem to
start the next became more a case of responding the mood of the line or
taking it as a signpost. It was as if the poems became like ambient music
in that they became atmospheres or environments that seemed able to
contain whatever I wanted them to.

Part 3 of The President... *is for me a quirky voice play, where a lot of very
interesting poetry is almost disguised by the allocation of it to different voices;
I wanted to just read some parts of it, to let various sections stand on its own.
You call it 'An Entertainment', a strange, slightly antiquated term these days.
Can you tell me how the piece was written?*

The impetus for 'Gardens' comes from a number of places. I became very interested in the Renaissance, fascinated by court masques etc. So the subtitle probably comes out of that. In fact, I hope it describes the fact that 'Gardens' is serious fun as opposed to just being quirky. I've also been doing a lot of reading of and thinking about pastoral recently too, particularly in terms of trying to understand how it's surviving. Some people argue that pastoral survives in environmental and feminist ecological writing. But it seems to me that one way it's surviving in poetry is self-reflexively, so that you get a kind of meta-pastoral going on. As I said earlier about mourning and remembrance, not just "doing" a genre but exploring its implications, even its practicalities.

The piece began as a series of notes and lyric fragments and just grew out of that. The "call and response" section which ends it—'Garden of rhetoric instruct us', "Garden of retirement entangle us"—was actually written first with the idea of having a section that explored each type of garden. But I decided this would be overdoing it; and I hope that the three gardens that are explored—'Love's Etcetera', 'State's Mirror' and 'Soul's Ease'—suggest a way of thinking about other meanings of gardens. The history of gardens and what philosophers and writers have taken them to mean is absolutely fascinating. When you go into it you find that gardens have always been tightly bound up with ideas of nation and nationalism and selfhood. There's a couple of great books Pluto Press brought out in the 1990s called *Gardeners Delight* and *Bread And Roses* by Martin Hoyles. The second one is a survey of gardening books which shows how political ideas got remodelled in horticultural terms. And I was struck by the fact that the image of the garden and gardeners is of individuals working alone and yet there's all these other voices literally clamouring away in the background. I couldn't conceive of it not being "broken up" as you call it.

You run a small press called The Cherry On The Top; and you've recently begun editing and publishing a magazine about poetry and poetics called The Paper. *Can you tell me more about these activities?*

The Cherry On The Top Press began for two reasons. First, because I often produce work which I want to get out into the world quickly to people who I think might be interested or pleased to receive it. Second, because I produce a lot of work which falls outside the usual definitions of poetry and which I can't imagine anyone else wanting to publish in the way I want to publish it. Some of the poems in part 2 of *The President of Earth* were first published in *The Elephant's Typewriter*; but the remainder I published in *Cities* which was an A3 folded card, a kind of poetry tabloid. The next thing I did after that was *Four True Prophecies Of The New State* which I guess comes under what people call visual text and was a response to turn of the millennium anxieties as well as to people finding an image of the Virgin Mary in a bag of pork scratchings and to the myths about Princess Diana that are all over the internet. That was first published as a set of four A5 printed cards; and is now in a second edition as four printed A4 sheets in a plastic folder. It includes a gospel based on aspects of the Diana myths; and a cut-up of Nostradamus. After that, I brought out my book on alien abduction, *The Fiery Chariot*, which is in the style of a seventeenth-century pamphlet and mixes texts and graphics and even has a music hall song in there. The Cornell pamphlet, *C: A Circuition Around His Circumambulation*, which Alan Halsey published with his West House Books imprint, was originally a handmade artists book published in a limited edition for the 2000 London Artists Book Fair. I've recently published a newly-discovered Cold War document, *Spook Rota*; and the first two instalments of a part-work called *Teach Yourself Criticism*.

The press doesn't just function as a personal vehicle. I publish things by other people which don't seem to fit easily into the usual categories. For example, Stephen Vincent's *A Walk Toward Spicer* is a short but highly resonant prose piece which literally retraces Jack Spicer's regular Sunday walk around the North Beach area of San Francisco; but also manages to say something about his ideas of creation being a process of dictation from outside the self. Later this year, I'll be publishing *A Pocket Dante* which is a collaboration between myself and Bill Herbert.

I've been thinking about doing a magazine for years but I've never been very convinced by the rattle bag approach to poetry magazines because hardly anyone's work gets shown to its best advantage. There's got to be a better way of doing things which is why *The Paper* has themed issues; only publishes invited work in an attempt to get a group of like minds together; and aims to give contributors quick answers and useful feedback during the editorial process. It seems much more interesting and valuable to get a group of people writing on pastoral or performance or lyric because there's a chance you might tap into things that are circulating in the larger culture. That's certainly happened with the current issue—no. 5—which is mainly devoted to elegy. And, of course, you find that different contributions play off and inform each other in surprising ways and therefore do something that's more like our wider experience of reading, writing and thinking.

[*Stride*, 2002]

Poets I Go Back To

HERE

What
has happened
makes

the world.
Live
on the edge,

looking.

I can still remember the mental and emotional lurch I got from this poem of Robert Creeley's when I first read it. Like many of his others it seemed to me, in its minimal musicality and language, crystal clear and lucid, even profound. It still does: this verse is typed up and blue-tacked to the wall in my study. I've passed on the individual Creeley volumes I used to have (something I regret!) and bought the *Collected Poems*, but I still read these early poems as they chart the fizz and jumps of thought in response to the world around us. Although the poem above, my favourite Creeley poem, isn't from it, I particularly like the occasional poems in *Hello: a Journal*, which range from minuscule works constructed from a rearranged song lyric on the radio, to longer poems and meditations, all immediate and engaging.

Creeley wasn't, however, where I started reading poetry, although he was soon after. And out of all the poets I'm going to mention here, he and Gavin Selerie are probably the only ones associated with the kind of poetry I prefer these days, which is in the main, for want of a better term, "linguistically innovative" and often American. But I've taken "poets I go back to…" to mean poets I've returned to for a good number of years, those poets who first enticed and challenged me, who originally opened my eyes to poetry, and whose books are still not only on my shelves, but frequently taken from said shelves to be re-read. So in this article I look back to my teenage years (and early twenties) in West London, and some well-thumbed volumes I still have from then.

T.S. Eliot's 'The Waste Land' is one of the few poems I remember my father reading. He read mainly non-fiction, and I wonder if his interest in London history was where he found a way in to Eliot's long poem? Despite studying the poem for A Level in the late '70s, I still don't "understand" some of the quotations or their point in the poem's scheme of things, I don't bother with the notes much; I am mainly still drawn to the incantatory and declamatory tones of the poem, the snapshots of people and place, the whole epic and panoramic nature of the poem. I still like "big" poems which attempt to grapple with life, the universe and the overall scheme of things: I'm currently working my way through Olson's *Maximus Poems* and exploring Rachel Blau DuPlessis' *Drafts* as she slowly adds, here and there in magazines on- and off-line, to her ever-expanding project.

Two other London books have stayed with me. First up is the original self-published edition of *Fox Running*, Ken Smith's fractured urban long poem. We start by meeting

Fox
running
loose in his sleek skin
loose in his slick fur

as he lopes from suburb to suburb, darkness to light, one moment to the next. What a surprise it was to find a poem written about my city, about stations and places I knew about, in everyday language. A poem that articulated doubt and angst, the edginess of contemporary living in the Thatcher years—I love the way the poem gradually spirals inwards through desperation, contemplation and self-doubt, then uncoils outwards in the final paragraph:

He is anyone wandering back
from the laundromat late Saturday noon

and leads on to the edgy, unnerving final line:

who all belongs to this blood then?

If Smith's poem was of the moment, Gavin Selerie's *Azimuth*, published four years later in 1984, and purchased at the long-gone Riverside Studios bookshop in Hammersmith, was more a retrospective sequence from the late '70s, featuring life as lived by the generation before me. These poems document the imploding counter-culture around Notting Hill and Portobello Road (at least the last two sections of the book do), a world I had only been on the edge of as I searched for bootleg tapes in Portobello Road and drank pints in The Portland Arms near my friend's house. Personal experience and diary poems interweave with political insight & opinion, poems about what the author was reading or listening to at the time, and poems rooted in place and transience. They too were an insight into how poems might be constructed, how the confessional and personal might be changed and used, how everyday language and life might be transformed, how poems could be knitted together into sequences that self-referenced and worked accumulatively.

Years earlier, I'd bought another poem sequence that has remained important to me, but *Crow* works in a totally different way. It builds a myth out of rough-hewn language, depicts a pagan world view drawing on creation and trickster tales from around the world. It's dark and cynical humour was mine in the mid '70s—all schoolboys then cultivated this cynicism, along with a Monty Python type humour. I heard Ted Hughes read from the sequence in St Peter's church in Hammersmith, and will never forget it; I also have a double LP of him reading the complete sequence (although the recent *Collected Poems* gives the lie to the completeness). Whenever I hear his rich warm voice, I am transported back to the fading evening light in that church, the hard pews, the traffic noise outside, and the huge man at the front declaiming his poems. Religious experience? Oh yes.

But the poems still work on the page for me. Their language is descriptively and emotionally rich, their stories still fresh and new, their theological insight still challenging and valid, their poetic and mythic power undiminished. I have no time for the current critical opinion which says Hughes' mid-period writing—*Crow*, *Cave Birds* and *Gaudete*—is his weak period. It isn't; this work towers above the nature poems or the lamentable offerings from when he was Poet Laureate. *Crow* is Hughes' masterpiece, and it's one of the few poetry books I often take a copy of with me on holidays or journeys (the slimline Faber 1999 reissue). I'm also lucky enough to have been given a limited edition hardback with drawings in by Baskin, something I take out and delicately finger my way through every so often.

Someone else I heard read, and who also wrote about magic and myth, though from a very different perspective, was Hughes' friend Peter Redgrove. On this occasion, he read, I believe, with Frances Horovitz, at the Orangery in Holland Park. My friend, the writer Brian Louis Pearce, had invited me along to one of an occasional series at the venue. It is Redgrove's early Selected Poems, *Sons of My Skin*, which I bought there and often return to.

In its pages we meet a creator who regards creation as a transitional experiment. In 'The Case' the narrator has some kind of mystical/natural epiphany:

And I swam in the thunderstorm in the river of blood, oil and cider,—
　　　—and so this mother-world
Opened around me and I lay in the perfumes after rain out of the river

These are themes Redgrove would return to time and time again over the years, where scent and touch and smell trigger sexual and other releases:

And it was like a door opening in the sky, it was like a door
　　　opening in the water,
It was like the high mansions of the sky, and water poured from the
　　　tall french windows
It was like a sudden smell of fur among the flowers, it was like a
　　　face at dusk
It was like a rough trouser on a smooth leg.

But all is not light and joy and happiness. We also meet the "Decreator":

Grown-up idiot, see the slow-motion of him,
And that slow-motion sludge of a tongue
Coiling along its stream of happenings,
Head lolling and tongue lolling,
Sudden brightenings, lurches.

as well as the gnostic minister of 'The Sermon', and a resurrected Lazarus, unhappy to be back in the world. Redgrove's pagan, pseudo-scientific universe has stayed with me over the years [indeed I've been fortunate enough to publish his work], but *Sons of My Skin* is less-focused and obsessive than later volumes, wider-ranging and more accessible. It's magical—in the truest sense of the word—world is a place I often return to.

Adrian Mitchell might baulk at my saying this, but his poems also offer another magical world, a utopian socialist vision, where things are hunky dory and everyone is equal. I used to go and see Mitchell read every couple of years, simply to hear him bringing his poems to life. On the page, I sometimes find them simplistic and naïve, but softly declaimed by the author they were wonderful, liberating and hopeful poems, even as they focused on and ranted against racism, war, violence and oppression. I especially remember one reading at the Young Vic theatre, where Mitchell read among what looked like the complete contents of the theatre's props cupboard, piled high on the stage. He sang, he chanted, he pleaded and he convinced. It is this voice that has stayed with me over the years. Like Julian Beck's *Songs of the Revolution*, which could be regarded as the anarchist version of Adrian Mitchell's socialist poems (interestingly, both were also involved in alternative theatre), I return to Mitchell's poems despite the poetry. They are part of my personal political development and history, part of my poetical and general education; a reminder of who and what I once was, and perhaps of what politically and socially might have been:

> when the revolution comes
> you will be standing at the prow and the salt wind blows in your face
> for hundreds of years you dreamt of the ocean
> now you are wet
>   (from 'Songs of the Revolution 86', Julian Beck)

[*The North* 34, 2004]

Ordering & Shaping

RUPERT LOYDELL INTERVIEWED BY BRIAN LOUIS PEARCE

BRIAN LOUIS PEARCE: *You see creativity as moving things round, I think? Trying it, seeing what happens. Starting with everyday life: what you see and feel, experience (as in regard to rites of passage, e.g. what you read and what you think as well as whom you meet and respond to or come up against)?*

RUPERT LOYDELL: I don't think I'd be alone in seeing my writing as a synthesis of what I experience. I like to think my work also focuses on language itself, which I believe is really how we experience, and indeed even create, the world around us. We can't possibly write about what we haven't in some way experienced or encountered—even when we write fiction we can only draw on that.

How do you see creative "play" working for the artist/writer?

I'd see it as learning to handle the stuff they use to make what they make. Playing with words, syntax, rhythm, visual layout for a poet all helps the writer understand how language works. I also see play as part of what I do, and playfulness.

Eliot talks about finding the objective correlative to channel/embody/utilise the initial emotional impetus by shifting it into something else and finding a form for it (or allowing it to find its own form), at which point it may become "art" or "artefact".

It is not unlike what the sculptor (Hepworth, perhaps) does with a block of stone, a pattern of seaweed, a pile if pebbles. It can be the found thing. But I am thinking more of the way we use experience as a starting block for ratiocination and application, producing something very different from it, but based on it, perhaps sparked by it. You find things and move them around. Play, try trial and error, but combined with analysis and reflection; making a long list of possibilities as it were, as a chess player might, then sorting out what works best for you. It seems to work for you.

Yes, I'm interested in pattern and form. The shapes I've invented or borrowed for my poems don't strike me as that much different from traditional rhyming or syllabic forms. I often use visual shape, word and line count, or alphabetical devices to structure my poems. I'm not that concerned with "play" beyond the fact that I find language pliable and exciting medium, one which I think a lot of people ignore the possibilities of.

You read a great deal, all the interviews with you bring that out; and you think about it, relate and associate; give us a good many references, implicit or noted. This can be great but I remember Gavin Ewart once cautioning me against the use of too many proper names and references in one's poetry. He felt it could create a barrier, deny access to some readers and create a private world. We can none of us read everything and we can feel second rate and marginalised by the sense of being "unlearned".

Let me stop you there! I put books down as "sources" in my recent books simply as a kind of nod towards acknowledging where I have often found phrases or ideas, not as any way of showing off.

The whole purpose of our art is to touch common chords, is it not?

No, I don't go along with that. That seems the way to lowest common denominator poetry; and I've no time for rhyming doggerel or such like, which is where that path ends.

You don't go in for the bardic idea, then, that the scop or minstrel crystallises the aspirations, griefs, rites, celebrations of the community? Admittedly not too many poets perform this function today in western society, partly because the religious and cultural consensus of earlier centuries has broken up.

I think you've kind of answered your own question, because I don't think the poet fulfils this role any more. I suspect our comedians or pop stars are today's minstrels and bards, not the poets. Poetry has become something else; society has changed. Having said that, I'd probably argue that what good poets write of course reflects the society they are part of and the world they live in—it can't do otherwise. But our world is fragmented and less communal than ever before, which may be why we need lots of different types of writing and song.

Rupert Loydell & Brian Louis Pearce

I'd be with Christopher Ricks in seeing Bob Dylan as a contemporary bard, but one might also cite Patrick Kavanagh and Seamus Heaney in an Irish context and, admittedly a few years back, the New Zealanders A.R.D. Fairburn and James K. Baxter. (This leaves open the meaning of "western" if it is not music or film but society! As an old timer myself, I'll settle for The OK Corral and what I used to hear on Folk on 2. That's misleading, of course, because it's nostalgia, largely, and not dealing with contemporary society at all, yet can embody myths which still pack potency.)

I'm afraid I don't know the New Zealanders but the Irish poets you mention may function in that way, yes. You probably agree that Irish culture is different? Also, is there a difference between being popular and bardic? I mean Les Murray is certainly touted as being popular in Australia, but I'm not sure he functions in the way you suggest in your original question. Dylan is interesting, too, and certainly is still popular—though more with the over 40s I think. Isn't his work to do with *song* though? I mean it's his words and music *together* that make his work important (or not). I can't see his lyrics as great poetry I'm afraid, although they certainly tap into some big themes and stories. But I wonder if they don't work in this mythical wild west way anyway? The idea of the frontier man, the rebel, the outsider, somehow having knowledge of society yet being apart from it? Anyone with a romantic streak is still drawn toward this outsider role, aren't they? Most poets in fact!

However, I think you are right about cultural consensus being broken up, or not existing, so that it's very hard for one person, or music group or whatever to speak for all. In fact Dylan has never spoken for all, he just spoke for a lot of people—if one was being cynical one could argue that that was fashion and hype as much as talent or relevance. Even Ted Hughes lost the plot a bit as Poet Laureate didn't he? Simply because many people aren't the slightest bit interested in the royal family or such like. And of course when events such as 9/11 happen which do provide a consensus of opinion, or certainly a media event, for most of the population, it seems that the arts are somehow inappropriate or not up to the enormity of the task.

Great answer, if I may say so! Yet I do sometimes feel with your work that I'm solving a crossword puzzle. In your attention to syllables and words, the letters that compose them, and the words' meanings, ideas and the response to experience can be lost. Maybe it's the way your critics discourse about semantic and morphological empathy, surrealist ethnography and the like?

All I'm trying to do in my recent work is order and shape ideas, but also allow the reader to construct their own poem. I think my structures reflect the way we think, which isn't in a linear fashion, but by skittering all overt the place, in a strange network of leaps, bounds and regressions. My poems hover around and above a theme or idea, throwing associative matter, themes, ideas and images into a patterned whole, and—hope—slowly allowing the poem and reader to move along.

But I'm not interested in dictating something, even "telling", the reader something. That seems to me to somehow hold the author up as having something to say; I'm more interested in discussing and sharing something with the reader.

I think you make it sound much more academic and difficult than my work is. It's a poetry of association and images, not some difficult avant-garde work. I have to say when I read the new work at readings people don't seem to have a problem with it, simply because I don't present it as problematical. I think my work is concerned with the same themes my writing always has been; it simply goes about dealing with it in a different way.

I don't feel we poets have any "need" to do anything. Poets and writers make things with language; that's what poets do. I'm not a lecturer, philosopher or storyteller, I'm a poet and I'm interested in exploring this marvellous thing we use everyday called language.

Your poems on your father are very moving. Is there not something about their style as well as their subject from which something is to be learned? And not only from your involvement/engagement, arguably?

Yes, they are moving. Yes, I admire their simplicity and clarity. It's not, however, what I'm interested in achieving at the moment, or how I write anymore. They seem like poems by someone else. I've written about death more recently, and used the way I write now to do so, in a—I believe—just as moving way. They strike me as somehow too confessional and experiential—that the narrator/poet has something important to share, and the reader empathises and is moved by them. They are genuine, heartfelt poems, and I'm glad people like them, but they aren't mature Rupert Loydell poems.

Having said that, they and other poems about death and dying, are in a book manuscript, *The Smallest Deaths*, which is currently out looking for a publisher.

'Fool's Paradise' and the sequences in Frosted Light *still please me a lot, though I have read them over many years of course, and they needed getting into at the time.* Dark Angel *and* Quartet, *for example, still seem to me very good indeed—and you were only 21 and 27 then! They are short but create sequences that shimmer and involve the reader, seem both exciting and to speak where we all are in question and feeling. Yet have their own order.*

You still stand by these sequences, I think, but in what way do you think you've improved, matured and shifted, experimented, since then? Are there other words than those you yourself would have put in this question?

Actually I think I see those as almost juvenilia. *Dark Angel* seems to me to rely far too much on Ted Hughes' *Crow* book for form and inspiration; I prefer *Quartet*, which was interesting to write, drawing as it did on various themes and ideas, and looking to the small poems of people like Robert Creeley for inspiration.

I think since then I've simply got to understand what you can do with language more. Andy Brown and Tony Lopez, particularly, one as a friend and one as an MA tutor, both introduced me to new poets and poetry which totally shook me up as regards these possibilities. I think I've learnt to allow the reader to make the poem with the author, and to not try and "tell" the reader something. If I have "something to say" then there are better ways of doing it than writing poems for the few hundred who might read my work.

I think the important word that's missing from your question is *changed*. More and more I believe we must be open to change. Writers must read, explore, try things, open themselves up to language. Language can befuddle, delight, bemuse, amuse, intrigue, exasperate—when it's used to tell shaggy-dog type narratives, with some kind of epiphanic ending, its just dull and boring. I'm still endlessly excited by writing. I read more and more, buy more and more books, find things online. I want to find out what other authors are doing, what is possible with this word stuff we use every day.

You place a high value on the linguistic elements of the poem artefact yet appear to discount the success of the word-and-sound play and felicitous verbal effects that (without drawing attention to themselves) convey the thought/feel so effectively in many parts of Quartet. *The clarity-cum-sparseness of certain sections is absolutely "spot-on" and stands the test of time. One has to move on, yes, but by denigrating this as "juvenilia" you could appear to be justifying our friend William Oxley's tenet that a poet is not the best judge of his own work!*

No I don't! I still use all the poetic devices available to me, whenever I need or choose to use them. I work particularly hard on the sound of my poems, so I think you're missing something here. Read them aloud! You're also being slightly disingenuous, as I seem to remember you didn't like Quartet when it came out—it's taken a long time for you to warm to it! In another ten years you'll perhaps like what I'm doing now!

Sequences interest you, obviously.

I often write in sequences because I set myself writing projects. Sheila Murphy encouraged me to think about making poems parts of things, be it short series, pamphlets or manuscripts, rather than "occasional poems"; to consider the bigger picture. So I still often work in sequences. I also find myself making variations upon a theme, coming at something from several angles, or wanting to play with a form in all its possibilities, which a sequence allows.

I haven't written another Easter sequence, if the subject matter of Quartet was part of the question, but I continue to write poems about faith & doubt, the (im)possibilities of belief today.

Have you thought of adopting personae, as of course you do in Dark Angel, *but perhaps in the more direct way that Browning or Clemo might, that is in a subject's voice as a "dramatic monologue"? Or one might address some other person or artist, as I do in my Giacometti sequence?*

Well, I learnt a long time ago that the narrator in any poem is usually a fictional character anyway! I don't trust this idea of the confessional poet pouring his heart out—he or she has already created something else. I think a lot of my poems invent personas, narrators; many certainly explore work by other artists, authors and people. The three 'Ballads of the Alone' all deal with not only concepts of photography and images, but specific photographers who are named, and their work. My prose poem, 'Shadow Triptych' explored the work of Francis Bacon; a recent poem drew on a newspaper story about Bono of U2 flying home each night from the band's tour to sleep beside his dying father—people assume the poem is me harping on about my dad again, but it isn't, it's an assumed voice drawing on a real-life story.

I think if people look, there are characters and narrators, explorations of specified or unspecified people of all sorts, in my work.

'House of Gloom', 'River of Death', 'Further than we Thought', are moving poems. This kind of honed brevity and surface simplicity suits you and the reader, and many another poet, I suspect. But isn't easy to write necessarily. Often one pares it down from a larger draft, doesn't one?

Actually just about all my work gets into shape quite quickly. My editing—and there are many edits, usually for 2 or 3 months on a daily basis—are more to do with twitching about small changes: punctuation, line length, vocabulary and such. I rarely start with a huge poem and then whittle it down. These kind of poems start small and lean and stay that way.

I know you are drawn to this kind of work, but I want to repeat that they are written in the same kind of way as what you perceive as my more difficult work. They are often collaged, they often contain assumed voices, asides, associative matter, and aren't necessarily to do with me confessing or sharing. They usually work with or around a core theme or idea - often the result of something specific (but this may simply be something seen, heard or read about). It's usually this idea I want to explore, rather than having something to tell the reader. I want the reader to explore the theme with me, be drawn in to a discussion about, say, death, getting older, or the nature of photography. I want them to enjoy the music, vocabulary, shape, rhythm and visual presence of the poem—more than any traditional notion of content.

It's true that the more poems show that they are "human", and are about some recognizable situation, locale, person or mood, (or use this as a springboard perhaps), the more they work for me and I can relate to them. The closely cerebral and analytic, referenced poems seem artificial by comparison at times, but maybe its me a generational thing, or simply the fact that it can take time to come to terms with any new work.

Poems can't be human, they are an arrangement of words on the page! Personally when things get too closely referenced, naming streets or characters and such, that's when I feel shut out of a poem. I also think people use such notions as a kind of emotional shorthand, invoking Dickens, Chaucer, Francis Bacon, who/whatever, instead of attempting to invoke or evoke the emotion anew.

None of my poems are "referenced" in a kind of academic way. The books I read, and I do read a lot, are an important part of the way I navigate through (or get lost in!) the world around me. They are simply part of what gets shaken down into my writing. I tend to think of myself as a sieve with lots of "stuff" (books, experiences, art, music, correspondence, events, etc) put in the top, then shaken through into the poetry I write. There's no formal sense of doing research or finding out about things for a poem—my poetry is heartfelt.

What determines the value of a work of art is the degree of its "inner necessity", Kandinsky says. And the degree to which we stick with it; don't give up too soon, get off the train too soon—as he puts it in a marvellous image—but keep pushing it around as we know Beethoven and Picasso did (and Yeats and Dylan Thomas, for that matter), not being satisfied too easily.

I'm not sure we can value art in this way. A poem or painting may be important to us at a certain point in time, or for a specific place. I'd rather hear Roger McGough being funny if I have to go to a poetry reading than endure most poets reading what has been made for the page, but it doesn't mean I think Roger is the best poet on the page; I might not want to spend much time with his work at home. How can a poem tell us how long it's maker has spent on it? There are criteria we can use to discuss and explore a poem or painting, but for me they don't usually involve content as a starting point, and there is little point in, for instance, applying the wrong rules to something that has been made. No point in wanting end-of-line rhyme in a concrete poem, for instance.

I think we have to start with the notion that what we are offered to read or look at has been made with the best intention, and that every mark/colour/gesture, every word/phrase/line/poem is as the painter or poet has chosen. We can then start criticizing, but all too often we are actually dealing with taste and what interests us at any given moment.

At the moment I'm interested in sequences of linguistically-innovative poems. I am exploring Rachel Blau DuPlessis' *Drafts*, Robert Sheppard's *20th Century Blues*, Tony Lopez's radical sonnet sequences in *False Memory*. Then again, I've just discovered the work of rob mclennan in Canada, who works in a much looser—or seemingly looser—way, which has given me some new things to think about: the shape a poem might take, for instance, on the page. Ten years ago I was reading something else; ten years down the line, I'll be reading something else again. The work I've just named will no doubt still be on my shelf, but it may not have the same importance to me it currently does.

I don't think notions of genius, or a set canon, are at all helpful. What we perceive as "great works of art" are all to often bound up with fashion, gender, race, money and such, usually in an historical way. That doesn't mean Picasso isn't an important painter; it does mean we only know about him and his work because of various things that have happened which have led to the value (artistic and monetary) we accord his work and their place in museums.

Sticking or not sticking to something is a personal decision. I am someone who works hard at what I do, other people write differently—sometimes keeping first drafts—but produce interesting and accomplished work.

What gets you writing, and who's it for?

I think that I write as a way of sorting out the world around me: noting it, documenting it, recording it, seeing how it, or I, ticks. I then choose some of my work to enter the public arena via exchanges and dialogues with friends around the world, magazines, booklets and eventually books. There is private work I produce and choose to keep private. Usually because I don't think it's good poetry, not because it is of a private nature.

The 'Ballads of the Alone' are very strong and spare, actually, perhaps giving the lie to some of my misgivings about the cerebral distancing elements. The engagement, the chorus like repetition, works well. But much of A Conference of Voices *might be called "ghost-writing" it is so dense with allusions and sources.*

Well, what's wrong with being dense and full of things? Why can't poetry be difficult? Surely it might continue to engage the reader and give up new things each time it's read? Your construct of my poem is probably very different to someone else's, which I think is brilliant.

Sometimes people make things more difficult than they are though! The first 'Ballads' starts with a very obvious image of the towers collapsing on 9/11; the poem moves from there to discuss ideas of media and image. The italicised lines are there to remind the reader this is only language, this is language, this is how we make sense of the world, how we make the world; the chorus/refrain reiterates an important point about photography and image. Around that we can start to deduce strands of argument and discussion. The whole thing is propelled along by the relentless rhythm of the piece. It works well at readings, although I often select just a few sections to read.

Do you see yourself as belonging to the establishment or the outsiders? The big show or the small? In worldly terms the bigger the show we belong to the better. The Catholic writer and artist has a fair-sized catchment from which he/she can find readers and common ground, and can draw images from the liturgy that others of us may lack. Yet the non-Catholic writer can draw images from quietness, bare walls, a simple meal (say) that may be equally valid. You regard all this as irrelevant, I expect?!

I don't have any agenda of finding common ground, I write—indeed, can only write—about what I experience, find and know. I don't believe I use difficult words or anything that people can't understand if they want to. I do rather think there has been a huge shift away from previously established metanarratives in the West towards a more diverse set of narratives and myths, a much less common common-ground. I think this simply means we have to think harder if we choose to use images and myths whether people understand what we take for granted. I am constantly finding children who don't know the stories of, for instance, Adam & Eve, Noah's Ark, Jacob's Ladder. On the other hand they know all about Diwali and it's festival of light. I don't think we can assume that we can use this idea of common ground as a shorthand any more; we must work afresh and find new ways to express things.

I think everything is up for grabs as images. Anyone may be moved by the sea, a quiet room, or a simple meal; that doesn't seem to me to be much do with liturgy or whether someone is a Catholic or not. It's what the writer does with those images that counts, surely? In the end all we are left with is the words on the page in front of us.

As for establishment or outsider, I've worked quite hard to try and tear down what Andy Brown terms the binary oppositions that are presented to poets at the moment. Most poets in the UK sell a few hundred of their books, very few are are establishment in that way at all. Most of us simply want more readers. I think people have every right to write the kind of

Rupert Loydell & Brian Louis Pearce

poetry they do, but a lot of it doesn't interest me, and I am tired of people saying "this is the only poetry that matters". I want variety and openness, which is different from saying I want it all on my bookshelf.

I used to think there were conspiracies afoot in the publishing world, now I just think there are market forces some people choose to be bound by. I also know there are fairly obvious routes and ways of getting reviews in various places—one simply has to buy the right people drinks or talk to them on the phone often enough, basically attract their attention. If this kind of notice is important to you then you will go schmooze; personally I prefer to keep in touch with people around the world and have open, frank and opinionated discussions about poetry and books.

But obviously I'm as pleased as punch when a major magazine publishes or reviews my work—but it's not the be all and end all of my ambitions. I also enjoy successful readings, when the audience is engaged and enjoys what I offer them. I like it when people buy my books.

Would you agree The Importance of Being Earnest *has no "agenda", overt or implicit; that it is "play", purely and see that as its strength?*

No, I'd see it as a satire on class and relationships, which implies critique and mockery. I think it has a comic agenda also, which uses both visual and written/said puns. It also, as you do in your question, makes a statement about "entertainment" and an audience's expectations and own agenda(s)!

When you feel good (in head, heart or groin) isn't it easier and quicker to express this in paint—and isn't your excitement fairly easily felt/shared by the viewer? Why does one write (under the same impulse)? What is one hoping to achieve? Doesn't the need to be speaking about something get in the way of getting the emotion/initial impulse anchored/accessible/shared?

I don't tend to write when I feel good, I'm that cliché melancholic poet. It's easier to write when something upsets me or moves me negatively. I'm not sure I'd want to express excitement, I'd want to move beyond that to understanding and a more complex reaction. My paintings at the moment are pretty small, quiet contemplative pieces by the way—I think the viewer has to spend some time looking at them to engage. I suspect many of my poems are the same.

I'm trying to achieve a patterned grouping of words on a page which synthesizes together something about a subject I am interested in, or moved by (or both). I don't believe you can use any language and not be saying something, but if you set out to proclaim or tell people something I think you are in trouble straightaway. You are in the realms of polemic or propaganda, and I don't like either of those things.

"Concrete" or "abstract" patterned language texts test their own capacity to convey ideas and sensations. This you would see as stimulus and challenge, perhaps?

There are ways we can use language differently which will affect the reader, and make poetry different from prose or everyday speech. I believe we experience the world through language, so we can create experience and ideas and sensation in language, because that is how humans experience the world anyway. But I'm not sure I see my poetry in terms of sharing or recreating emotion or sensation, its more an exploration about something, which I hope the reader will create, or co-create, from the words and lines I offer them. As I've said elsewhere though, I don't want to dictate merely one simple reaction. I'm interested in the complexity of the world around us, and the possibilities of language itself.

Writing the fifty 15-line poems of Familiar Territory *was a useful discipline/a way of releasing what you felt/thought/wanted to say/finding and creating variety/unity/ simply an exercise? Which phrases or others most relate to how you see it?*

All of them except "simply"! More and more I plan what I want to try and do, try and think ahead to what I'm producing, rather than write "occasional poems". Even when I do write individual poems I'm constantly thinking about possible groupings of work into sections or whole books. Sheila Murphy gave a fantastic seminar at the Arvon course we co-ran, discussing this whole idea of looking ahead and thinking about what we were writing—is it a pamphlet? a book? a life's work? a long poem? or what? I've very much taken that on board.

I enjoyed typesetting Sheila's Stride book and was intrigued by her vocabulary. So I made a list of fifty words from it, decided on a flexible form (15 lines offers various possibilities of verse and line groupings) and wrote the poems. So the titles came first, and the poems came from those titles. But they are all to do with my life when I wrote them. There's no way what a person writes can't be! I had a discussion today with someone who was talking about people writing "academic poetry", but when pushed they couldn't name an example. People don't write deliberately obscure, difficult, or pretentious poetry; they write what they want and we have the right to engage with it or not.

Wouldn't it have been better to choose your own phrases or ideas?

Than what? I did choose the titles, I chose every word, phrase and piece of punctuation that went into the fifty poems. Each and every one of those poems is mine. My ordering, my words, my phrases—even if they are appropriated phrases, they are given a new context and meaning because I have put them alongside or with other phrases. Collage is only a working method, not an end in itself.

In what way does collaborating with others help you realise your own creativity—those elements that no one else can provide or have?

I love the push and pull of collaboration, the way poems are taken away from where you think they're going and you have to deal with that. I like being surprised, I like what the people I work and have worked with do with language, their ideas and methods. I've learnt to trust what is happening and "go with the flow"; and I like the discipline of projects underway, knowing that I have two lines, or whatever, to write to send back to Bob Garlitz or Roselle Angwin or whoever. That gives a certain sense of urgency or responsibility which focuses one. And I think writers write, so having projects like this underway keep the writing going.

You say that Peter Redgrove, for example, has something to say about faith (and I would say about the inspired character of life per se) in his poetry without any specific Christian belief. Can you give a few clues as what you (and he) mean?

I simply mean Peter explored the unseen and occult, but I believe with a certain detachment and an understanding of myth, ritual and sociology. These things inform our understanding of faith and belief; Christianity is rooted in myths and stories which have all sorts of connotations and links to other myths and stories, humankind's history since time began. If someone is sceptical about something it doesn't mean they don't understand it. Peter's knowledge about sexuality and the senses, how we experience the world, I rate as second to none.

He is optimistic, celebratory, would you agree?

Yes indeed. His is a delightful and totally original take on human experience. A kind of indulgence and wallowing in what many of us simply don't take note of. And I think he was far more comic and teasing than many seem to realise, not at all po-faced or dull. He delighted in life and his interpretation of it, which included invented fantasy, sexuality and ritual.

When you take phrases, words, slogans from magazines, adverts, songs or overheard conversations or your own notebooks, what is the associative/integrative process you are aiming at?

It differs I think. I may organise a poem through word count, syllabics, by the alphabet, by the number of lines, or through a theme or concept. In the end I think associative is the word—I believe that the phrases and interwoven language in my poems gradually builds up a web of allusion and intertextual and imagistic links which the reader can then assemble some kind of meaning from. That is unlikely to be a narrative or a coherent argument or statement. It is likely to be open-ended and not offer epiphany or transcendence as any kind of grand closing statement.

Do you weigh, shape or savour phrases for their sound's sake and to maximise these sound values (consonance/assonance and the total effect of a phrase or several phrases) 1. not at all; 2. for its own sake; 3. consciously but only in service, if not subservience, to the sense?

2 and 3. I rarely ignore the sense of what is being said [and as I said above, I don't think words ever don't mean anything], but yes I do pay attention to the music of the poem. Having said that I think many of us have our own sense of musicality in language. My friend Andy Brown finds a lot of my poems quite flat and unmusical; I think I hear a different voice in the poems to the one he does.

As a poet one considers all the possibilities open to us, but different poems at different times are constructed with a different main focus. Some poems pay more attention to what is being said than how it is being said, others are organized visually, others musically. I read all my poems out loud, although I write mainly for the page.

A writer like David Miller uses words and phrases sparingly; rather like Robert Lax's words are spaced on the page. This makes them count, arguably, more than in a hen-run of verbiage. How do you feel about that, and how does it relate to your own approach?

Rupert Loydell & Brian Louis Pearce

I think at the moment the "tesserae" that David offers the reader interests me more than his minimal approach. But I respect the care and precision of David's writing especially. Robert Lax's work I feel is more playful, and focuses our attention on the few words he has chosen, and the arrangements of those words on the page.

I think I'm working quite differently from Lax, certainly; both authors were probably far more of an influence a few years back, when I corresponded with both.

In your 'Ballads of the Alone' the refrain works to firm up the structure and to build an edifice against what destroys? Would you agree—to the first point anyway? If to the second, I presume it was instinctive, subconscious, but no less valuable for that?

Actually it's there to firm up the structure but also the content. It constantly makes the same statement, and gets the reader questioning how the parts of the poem interrelate on the given theme. They are a kind of footnote, a reminder, a constant throughout. I don't see the 'Ballads' being about what destroys though, they are poems discussing photography, faith & doubt, and our perception/representation of the world.

Do you give time to writing and painting pretty equally, these days?

I'm more of a writer these days, my domestic life means I write more than paint. But I still do both.

Does the one influence the other and, if so, how?

It's pretty indirect I think. Like the music that I listen to, I often feel that I absorb ways of working, the shape and composition of art, the structure of work, more than anything. I rarely explore the same things in my paintings and poetry at the same time, nor write from/about my paintings or vice versa. But I do feel that the way I write at the moment is much more how I paint than it used to be—I treat language and paint in similar ways, as very pliable and fluid mediums.

Have you thought of writing some prose: non fiction on art, say, or "theology" or something down to earth? Or fiction? I man as a change from poetry when you feel like writing something of responding to something but are not dramatically inspired? I share the work-ethic idea, but perhaps one should vary the genre, so as not to risk going stale. In your case the painting does this perhaps?

I think the collaborations and set projects do it for me actually. I also write reviews and articles, remember, and prose poems, which I regard as something quite different, too. I have never managed to write sustained prose, I'm simply not interested in narrative enough. And I don't want to reduce this idea of writers writing to "work ethic", its more to do with their engagement with language, which might only mean 5 minutes writing a day. It would certainly mean lots of reading though!

[...]

Do maths, science or astronomy influence your work? The idea of the maze?

I don't think any of those directly feed in. I feel things such as psychology, philosophy, theology, sociology and chaos theory have all changed the way we perceive the world, which means we must reassess how we write about them. If we understand to any extent the way we navigate our way through the world, then surely it will mean we have to change our writing to suit? I find the concept of linear narrative, for instance, strangely inappropriate for our complex world; ditto the straightforward confessional poem with some kind of neat epiphanic ending.

You won't give up the confessional/narrative poems, will you? They will be the better, though, for your linguistic experiments.

In a way I think I have. The poems you see in this way I know I have often written using the same processes as what you regard as more experimental work. I am very aware that the narrator of my poems is not the author of the work.

Your writing has attracted its due share of jargonised specialist criticism. This has the potential to be distracting, especially if a writer/subject allows his or her work to be pushed in that direction.

I think like all "jargon", or what gets accused of being jargon, there are things to consider. Firstly it's a specialist language, which doesn't make it pretentious, just something we need to find out about if we are interested in the subject it applies to. It's simply a kind of shorthand for discussing, so we don't have to keep explaining and re-explaining things.

Secondly, just as one doesn't expect to learn a foreign language without applying oneself, so why expect to immediately understand different linguistic and critical fields? Having said that I don't think anyone has written particularly turgidly or incoherently about my work. Personally I find it useful to have intelligent feedback.

How would you define "surrealist ethnography" in the poetic context? ("Scientific study of races" doesn't get us very far?)

I wouldn't. I think it's a surrealist term in itself. But you obviously know what ethnography is, or have looked it up and do now, so I'd like you to think about how that might work in a surreal manner. This seems to me an obvious example of where I have invented, or appropriated, a term I find intersecting, or amusing, and want the reader to conjecture the implication.

Juxtaposition/association of previously unrelated concepts remains the bedrock of a post-futurist-surrealist art, I posit. Discuss.

I wouldn't want to be associated with futurism, which seems to me implicitly fascist; and I'm not actually a great believer in much of surrealism once it wanders into dreams and the subconscious. I simply think juxtaposition and association is actually how the human brain thinks. Instead of trying to present the reader with an answer, I'm interested in asking questions, meeting the reader earlier on in the thinking process. Working together to produce something.

Post- or whatever terms are only handy labels. But humankind does regularly find out more about how we think, why we do what we do, and what/why we can understand about ourselves. This affects the arts, the sciences, the media; everything. We can't pretend the world isn't different, or at least our understanding of it hasn't changed. I'm interested in trying to make poems that think about how we think.

As for bedrock, well I think with the invention of film, our traditional understanding of narrative was taken away. We began to understand (and this is obviously present in Joyce and Beckett, and in a more populist way Katherine Mansfield) narrative fragmentation and reject closure. We understand that we see the world in a fragmented way, not a linear way; and being aware of our minds flicking from thing to thing almost encourages us to think more obviously in that way, so media starts to work in that way, and on it goes in an ever-closing cycle.

This doesn't mean traditional novels or poems can't and aren't written; it probably means though that if we are thinking people then we understand "Once upon a time.../ ...happily ever after" stories as artifice. And of course we have actually seen the popular novel change—look at the success of someone like David Mitchell with his interlinked narratives. What you could perhaps argue is that it has taken the general public and mainstream critics a lot longer to accept some of these things in this country than in, say, Europe. It seems to me we are a lazy and conservative nation. Only now does it seem we are finally seeing the shake up of canons and lists to finally get to see and read the important poetic works that have been going on for forty or fifty years in the small presses. (I'm thinking of work by poets such as Allen Fisher, Tom Raworth and Lee Harwood.)

I was thinking of Boccioni's States of Mind triptych—'Farewells', 'Those who go', 'Those who stay'—with its simultaneous viewpoints and a sympathy for the human condition of his (and perhaps our) day. I can't see this as anything but original and reverberating art; anything but a political statement!

Well I think all art has a political context, but I would see the Boccioni paintings as having a lot more to do with cubism than futurism, with ideas of multiple viewpoints rather than the supremacy of machinery and power. It is perhaps where futurism has become diluted, and moved on from the rather fascist manifestos it issued? I mean, even the titles of the triptych paintings alert the viewer to the human presence as the subject matter. As you know, I saw one version of the triptych in Madrid, and very much enjoyed them. I remember alerting you to the fact that Tim Liardet had also used the work and some of the ideas in the paintings in his *God of Rain* book, as you did back in the 60s in your 'States of Mind' sequence when you were first struck by cubist, surrealist and futurist art.

Your work in A Conference of Voices *perhaps has something in common with the cubists and, in passing, with Tim Liardet, in the way you use multiple voices and viewpoints?*

Yes, I suppose so, although I think Liardet seeks more resolution in his poetry than I do: I find his work still rooted in self-expression and narrative closure, whereas my work remains more open and fragmented. I think

Liardet drew on certain aspects of Boccioni's work: the quotes Liardet has used as epigraphs show Boccioni's interest in humanising machinery and in turning the dynamics of both movement and sensation into "quasi-musical harmony". There's a sense here of trying to create order out of disorder, a unity out of the various, which I certainly think is part of my work.

Similarity in difference (variation in unity, the recurring if altered motif) is a crucial and formative notion. The composer does it all the time. We see it in my own Victoria Hammersmith *and* Goldhawk Variations, *if I may say so. We see it of course in human beings, and in what we experience when we travel to different countries and/or cities. Perhaps the ethnography comes in here?*

The world is certainly more homogenized that when I first entered it. High streets are the same, cities are more and more alike, the small shop and hidden corner hardly exists any more. Mall culture has hit Britain big time! But on the other hand it is easier and easier to contact people via email, and have critical dialogue around the world, easier than ever to publish a book, or get people to read your poems (which isn't the same as selling a book).

Your novels seem to me different from the networks of meaning we have been discussing. *Victoria Hammersmith* seems to be an episodic novel, where meaning accrues as we understand and discover more and more about the subject. We also discover that she may not be remembering correctly, so the narrative is questioned from both within and without. *Goldhawk Variations* is similar in some respects, but also draws on the idea of the musical variation. But it is obviously clearly planned and worked over, it isn't—to take a musical analogy—the chance operations of John Cage; it's still working within mainstream composition.

The city is an interesting metaphor for poetry. I wouldn't want to push the notion of ethnography much further though!

We've both recently read Cole Swensen's online article 'Poetry City'. Do you agree with her that collage, juxtaposition, variation within unity/continuity, are crucial elements, together with pattern and sound phrasing in relating to the city, as is dashing movement, break up, remoulding, noise, confusion of scale and movement? is it this city-muse that you are aiming at, or something like it?

Well, it would rather be like fitting something to a mould afterwards, but yes it's a very useful article and idea. I certainly thrive on city life when

I'm there, and it is the prime example of disjointedness and juxtaposition, isn't it. Where else do we see people living in such a variety of ways? Where else is high and low culture seen side by side? Where else does media and hype and fashion rule, as beggars ask for 10p in front of neon hoardings? As the countryside becomes emptier and emptier, and towns and villages become suburbs, true cities seem to be the only real place where people are actually alive. Otherwise, like me, they order their music and books from the net, correspond via the net, and occasionally venture out to a homogenized pub or cafe to meet a few friends.

Is displaying the different person types of the city more important than or as important as the language and style?

No. I don't write about person types or about physical geography very much any more, although it's representation might interest me.

Would you emulate Roy Fisher's City *in modern terms, if you could? Perhaps you feel you have?*

Well I have you to thank for even knowing about *City* pretty early on. I think it inspired, or fed into, led me to, writing some early work about London and Coventry, but I'm not that interested in conjuring up Exeter for others. That doesn't mean other people couldn't do it though. But why would one want to emulate something? I mean read and read and read, yes, get ideas and inspirations, find ways of working, but I'd want to do something totally different.

Fisher was probably the first author I read who wrote prose-poems, too, which have become important to me.

So you wouldn't think of writing villanelles, say?

My initial reaction would be a loud "no"! I couldn't see the point, although slowing down, one can see there might be a playfulness in the form. Again, I might want to try and understand what villanelles do and subvert, or re-invent them. I wouldn't dream of stopping anyone using traditional forms, it's when people somehow think poems have to do this or that that I get cross—usually it means they have no understanding of poetry at all, just some vague notion of end-of-line-rhyme or a wish to self-express. Not to actually read and write poetry. We're back to language, I think, and finding ways to play and work with it, and make it work for us. I think it's difficult

Rupert Loydell & Brian Louis Pearce

to write a in the 21st century, or a sonnet; it's perhaps becoming difficult to write like Eliot or Auden—things have changed, including poetry.

Juxtaposition of fragments, angles, vignettes, bit like jigsaws that meet at angles at their edges but, in this case to invite academic exposition?

Yes, a jigsaw is a good analogy. Both I, as author, and the reader, assemble the work. But no, I have no interest in academic exposition. I'm not part of academic circles and have no particular wish to be—the current academic way of referencing references about references seems to me in the main tiresome and unhelpful. I do, however, enjoying reading about and discussing the whys and wherefores of how people write. Poetics isn't necessarily "academic"—plenty of it is perfectly readable and enjoyable.

How do you pattern your mosaic? Order your (found) dislocation?

Same as all poets do. By theme, association, sound, rhyme, assonance, word count, syllable count, visually, intuition.

Dislocation mirrors aspects of modern life, certainly. But is it not the privilege of art to both enjoy itself and bring some order out of chaos, put some pieces together? Any shaping does this, and can be art for art's sake or not, as you wish: it is not a case of being didactic.

Yes, I agree. All writers have put together their work, brought order to chaos. But that doesn't mean it has to "declare" something. I simply feel that when people think they have something important to say they are often deluding themselves, or that poetry isn't the means to do this. Much better to offer something than declare. Much better to see what language can do—the word and sound play you mention above, along with every other poetic device available to the writer.

Dislocation can form elements in a larger framework, of course, just as in jazz or sonata form music. Or do you resist bringing them into association or under this sort of control?

Of course not. I'm in total control of what is in my poems. Every poet is. One of the mistakes people make is by starting with the assumption that an author doesn't know what they have written. One has to start with the assumption that everything is deliberate and look for links and music and form, before criticising. I'm not, of course, suggesting there aren't bad poems.

Emotion must find its parallel, Eliot's "objective correlative" concept argues, yet the simplest statement: "I love, I mourn", touches the core still for most people. It is a truism that since Eliot's time, if not earlier, art for one's peers has tended to diverge from the "popular" or "I know what I like" variety. Do we ignore this factor? Or is not just in this that the art of large-scale piano variations (say)—to which I've referred earlier—has something to offer us?

The given theme is stated at or near the commencement of the piece; echoed, hurried or slowed, stated again in some obvious way, in recognisable relation to the original; restated at the close, usually eloquently, but in between there come variations which are as distant from the original in tempo, inversion, phrasing, atmosphere and emotion—that is, as difficult to identify as having any connection with the original—as the composer can manage. It is the second element that the composer and his peers may enjoy most but it is the whole that is significant to the performer and listener over the years; the whole that satisfies and thrills us, creates catharsis, in effect; and the whole which appeals to a wide range of people, and which balances both the recognisable and direct elements and those that are most distant but which derive from them.

Do you think you do this or something like it; try to achieve the same effect in your different way (how?), or aim at other goals (which?)?

Well, let's agree to disagree. I think it's very hard even in real life to use phrases like "I love you" any more, and on the page I think this kind of statement is redundant and simply lazy. There is much more to language than the simple statement, the narrative story or report.

I don't actually think poetry has ever been that popular, and even if it has been or could be, I think that the supposedly populist stuff being published today simply proves that it isn't at all interesting for the general public—it doesn't sell and it doesn't interest many people. Actually the poetry that interests people is the difficult stuff. Eliot's 'The Waste Land' still intrigues people, as does work by Pound, Olson, Berryman, and many others. It's not the lightweight stuff C. Day Lewis, Betjeman or Larkin offered us.

I think your exposition of piano variations is excellent, and I would immediately say that something like my 'Ballads of the Alone' do exactly this—circle and return to their given theme[s], with a very forceful musical statement in them. What worries me is your use of the word catharsis.

Rupert Loydell & Brian Louis Pearce

I also want to point out that music is essentially abstract, so if people actually understand how music works (and I don't think people do; they look for "tunes") then they know how to listen to any kind of music. It's a familiar problem though: people look at art for the story it tells, poetry for the content. If people bothered to read widely and understand how poetry works then we wouldn't have this nonsense about people finding it difficult, or claiming contemporary poetry is difficult. If people looked at the history of art and understood the medium of painting, and some of the concepts of 20th Century art, then contemporary art wouldn't be perceived as difficult. (Not that I think music or art or writing should necessarily be easy.)

Do you see yourself as conversing with your reader; talking, declaiming; pouring out a monologue, or something else? Do you have/invent a specific reader/ interlocutor for a particular piece?

I simply write what I want to and offer it to the readers in journals and books. The work can stand alone and find its place in the scheme of things. I know there are people out there who enjoy my work, I have correspondents and friends and contacts around the world who say so. I also have other correspondents who criticize and challenge, which is fine. And whenever I read my work aloud I meet new people, some of whom enjoy the work. But I wouldn't dream of thinking everyone will, or should, like my work; and, no, I don't write with an audience in mind, I simply write what I write then think about where it fits within my work, and where I might place it for publication.

[*Stride*, 2005]

Time Travel: *Andrew Poppy on Zang Tuum Tumb*

It's 2005. There's a beautiful blue and grey box set in a jiffy bag delivered to my door. It's a ZTT box set, featuring most of composer Andrew Poppy's recordings for the company; albums and singles, including an unreleased album. I've been looking forward to this for some time.

It's 1981, the beginning of the music decade we are told we love to hate. Somewhere and somehow rhythm, minimalism, krautrock and post-punk collide and Regular Music and Lost Jockey are born, two ensembles who specialise in energetic contemporary classical music. Andrew Poppy, co-founder of Lost Jockey, gives music critic John Gill a call at *Time Out* magazine, and also contacts weekly music newspaper *Melody Maker*.

RUPERT LOYDELL *Andrew, what did John Gill make of your music? I knew him more as someone championing jazz-rock, progrock, krautrock and experimental post-punk music. Did he have a clue about contemporary classical music? Was he surprised to hear from you? Did he like the music these ensembles were making?*

ANDREW POPPY John was very knowledgeable and open minded. He lives with the composer Graham Collier who does a kind of improvisation-meets-composition thing coming out of Mingus/Gill Evans. One of my best friends at University was the flautist/saxophonist Geoff Warren and he played in Graham's band. Then in 1980 Graham wrote a musical called *A Kind of Game* and I was roped in to play bass guitar in the small on-stage band. John was really into Kraftwerk and the way that repetition works in early minimal music was similar I think. It seemed obvious when Lost Jockey got going to contact him. He came and heard us and then give us a feature in *Time Out*. This led to John Leckie coming to one of our concerts at the Air Gallery and the ensemble going into Abbey Road.

It seems very obvious now, to use marketing and media in this way to attract new audiences, but I suspect it was quite unusual at this time, especially in the classical world. Did you feel ahead of the game? Did it do you any good in the short or long term?

Looking back I suppose I intuitively understood some-thing about presentation. If you want an audience at all there has to be some kind of communication strategy. I suppose some University composers, from the security of tenure, and the fact that the student body is a captive audience, might think that trying to create a popular platform for so called serious music damages the work. But historically this fracture between what is of serious value and what can have popular appeal is very recent. I mean Shakespeare was popular by all accounts. So there has to be a way of letting people know that something exists. We're not in a village situation where everyone knows what's going on. Catching people's attention becomes a very important job in the cycle of creating something and an audience experiencing it. Marketing is a necessary part of culture in mass society, you may as well deal with it creatively.

It's 1985 and Andrew Poppy is signed to ZTT, where Paul Morley and Trevor Horn hold court. Frankie Goes to Hollywood have put money in the coffers, and everything looks good.

Many people say the ZTT bands were simply used by Morley (media and hype) and Horn (production and session musicians) for their own ends, and eventually said bands, realising they were merely pawns in a musical marketing game, went belly up. But Poppy alone seems to have retained control—he was the only ZTT artist to produce his own records. And what records they were!

***The Beating of Wings**, his debut, is a beast of two parts. The first two tracks are pure orchestral energy, layers and layers of slowly changing lines pulsing and shimmering out of the speakers. Think Philip Glass and Terry Riley, think light sparkling hypnotically on a fast-moving river. Then 'Listening In' arrives, a work more concerned with rhythm than melody, and one assembled in the studio.*

Andrew, I have to be honest and say that, for me, 'Listening In' sounds of its time—more like Peter Gabriel meets Jon Hassell and jams with 23 Skidoo than what we'd expect from Andrew Poppy. [Actually that meeting of musicians sounds quite good!] Those awful rotatom and drum sounds are pure '80s. What do you think?

"I have to disagree with you on your police work there Pete."

It sound like you're not into 'Listening In', which is fine. But all the percussion sounds are custom-made samples put into the AMS and triggered from a sequencer. There's no synthetic drums. There's the Linn drum snare and bass drums which yes I can see now that does place it very much in the '80s. But all of the other percussion pattern are original sounds. I'm hitting the drum.

Obviously technology has moved on, and you were working with Fairlights and early drum machines. Would you make this track differently now?

It's got a unique sound that comes from the way it was put together. Impossible to reproduce.

The original album finishes with 'Cadenza for Piano and Electric Piano', an interesting piece where the electric piano slowly gains control of the piece, subverting both the sound of the acoustic instrument and the listener's expectations, since the piece begins as a gentle lilting tune yet moves toward repetition and echo. In fact, by the time it ends on a single note endlessly repeated it verges on being bloody annoying!

On CD1 of the box set, however, we move on to the first of several different versions/edits of pieces featured on the box set, the most important— and lengthy—of which is 'The Impossible Net', which revisits and reinvents '32 Frames', adding a new piano solo, playing with tempo, and generally working in the studio to collage and dub mix the music.

Andrew, you've talked about your idea of 'The Impossible Net' being a frame [or grid; a net even!] to hang sounds on, but one that starts to break down. Can you expand on that idea?

It's very simple variation form. (See Goldberg or Diabelli.) The chord sequence stays the same whilst the style and character of the music changes. The repetition of the sequence sets up expectation. One of the things about making repetitive music is that it has to have some internal tension to really work. So that you want to hear whatever it is repeated again. You can't just repeat anything. With '32 Frames/The Impossible Net' it's a classic device of the augmented 4th interval in the bass which means after just 4 chords you're sort of on the edge of a precipice. (It's the way the flute solo and the structure of Debussy's 'L'après-midi d'un faune' works.) Although this was reached in an intuitive way. I didn't sit down and say I'll have a tritone in the base. I'm sure with poetry you don't say I'll just invert this iambic foot. That's an analytic tool that comes later. Although I think that cooler reflecting has an important part to play in the process of making something.

Anyway 'The Impossible Net' tries to break down the inevitability of the repetition. It does this in two ways through the chance of tempo and the shift in the key. So after being lulled into the hypnotic state there are a couple of lurches which rip a big hole in the momentum. Like a curtain opening the machine makes way for the completely improvised fantasy on F minor. And a collaged one at that. I didn't make the piano solo to go there originally but I recognised that it was absolutely the right thing once I started working on 'The Impossible Net'.

In retrospect, it seems that you were just one of several individuals or groups of musicians becoming aware of the idea of the studio as instrument. Brian Eno and This Heat spring to mind, perhaps Peter Gabriel again. I mean Lee Perry and dub plates had been around a while but no-one seemed to have taken any notice. Then suddenly the intellectuals are lecturing on 'the studio', and every pop band has a 12-inch single out with at least one different remix on, preferably on coloured vinyl!

It's about the creative object losing its certainty under pressure from mechanical reproduction. Which is the real film, *Apocalypse Now* or *Apocalypse Now*, the director's cut? If it's the former what does this situation say about authorship? I know film's a bit different but even so.

Trevor Horn was obviously well ahead of the game in production terms. How much of an influence did he have on the way you worked?

He has high standards so you have to make it work. But he wasn't standing over my shoulder, just really encouraging. I wasn't new to making records or working with technology. We had a long conversation just after I was signed to the label where he started to talk to me about Tomita, a '70s Japanese musician who did versions of Debussy on synths. A kind of Wendy Carlos for 20th century music. I was a bit shocked because I wanted to make something more edgy and with musicians as well. 'Kink Konk Adagio' couldn't get further away really; it sounds so tribal.

I suppose because Trevor productions were always chasing the latest technology I was able to see what was going on, first hand. But the Fairlight wasn't new to me, I'd already done a big theatre project with it. But the Fairlight was very expensive and a big machine more like a

Hammond organ. I can't remember exactly but probably sometime in '87 Steve Lipson got a Compaq portable computer running an early voyetra sequencer. He could take it home. Immediately I wanted one. I'd always worked with programmers, like doing dictation, putting in the notes etc. I just wanted to be able to get hands on.

And Paul Morley? Were you happy to work with him on advertising and image? For me he is such a great mixture of bullshit, intelligence and wit! He was, probably still is, a big fan of Andrew Poppy?

I bumped into Paul again in about '98 at a party. He said something like "If I'd been running ZTT you'd be on your 16th album by now." But actually that period of the label was so strong because of the cohesion of a classic team: Jill Sinclair doing the business, Trevor having the musical visions and expertise, and Paul working on the presentation and images. And given that I was a kind of a law unto myself, if any of them had not been really interested in what I was contributing to the label then I'd have been out on my ear. If you read Ian Peel's article for *Record Collector* on ZTT you see how many acts were signed that never made a record. I feel very luck to have made two or three.

CD2 of the box set contains the Andrew Poppy album I treasure most, *Alphabed*—except it doesn't. Disappointingly, for me, it contains the 7-inch and 12-inch edits of 'The Amusement' instead of the complete version originally on the album. Never mind, it's still stunning stuff, and the two single versions make good aural bookends to this box-set version of the album.

'45 is' is a fast-moving 20-minute trance piece with slowly shifting repetitions and patterns with overlaid ensemble voices. Think minimalism, think loops, think high-energy systems music. Think masterpiece. Even better still is 'Goodbye Mr G', a moody low-tempo piece featuring Annette Peacock on sultry vocals and lots of rhythmic and percussive detail.

Dear Mr Poppy, whatever has happened to the complete/original album version of 'The Amusement'? Come on, defend yourself! I like it a lot; it should be on the box set. Yours sincerely, Mr. Grumpy of Exeter.

Dear Mr Grumpy, I'm really sorry. I thought that it worked much better with the two other versions enveloping '45 is' and 'Goodbye Mr G'.

When we were making *Alphabed* originally it was primarily for vinyl. CD was only just catching on. It's hard if you're making long pieces to deal with 25 minutes a side. There is actually an end section of '45 is' that we did live, which I cut, because it didn't make the record work. But I'm happy with that. It's interesting how Feldman has really flourished in the context of CD because it suits his long endless soft music. But he died before CD took off. PS Life's too short!

The final three tracks on CD2 are more revisits to 'Listening In', a kind of mini-[editing?]-suite. You were unhappy with the original by that time, yes?

It's partly that I was making a b side for The Amusement 12 inch. Also the way that the percussion was set up on the multi-track, there was an infinite number of mixes. In a way there always are. I was exploring something.

Are you happy with the work now? Which version is the final one of 'Listening In'? Or are they variations on a theme?

Never really completely happy but occasionally I have fun. I played 'Kink Konk Adagio' for people recently at a party and really enjoyed it. Yes, variations on a theme.

It's 1988. Paul Morley and Trevor Horn's version of ZTT is falling apart and Andrew Poppy's third album, *Under the Son*, is recorded but never released. The new box set contains, we are told, "the majority"—38 minutes; three tracks—from that album. The three tracks continue the trajectory of the first two: rock dynamics and minimalism combine to stunning effect. 'The Sequence' is not a million miles from 'Goodbye Mr G', but is much more uptempo; 'The Passage' seems to me a more successful take on ideas first found on 'Listening In'. But here much of the percussion is real, not sampled or electronic; the elastic web of rhythm stretched and pulled, compressed and deformed, before bouncing back to its original shape. Sounds appear and disappear— the sleeve notes highlight a cello sound replaced by a pneumatic drill, which is then slowed to become a kind of drum roll. This may sound tricksy, but this is Poppy, or compiler & commentator Ian Peel, telling us something that isn't actually what we hear. Well, it is, but we don't note it as such. I hadn't noticed any drill samples, simply the intriguing musical changes, with constant returns to a sung chorus, which occasionally itself becomes transformed into breathing or grunts. It's definitely another studio composition!

The album, and indeed the box set, finishes with 'Sometimes It Rains', a lumbering, almost progrock finale. Apparently built from samples, it clatters and honks & hoots its way along like King Crimson at their very best, before the drums drop out of the mix and leave the other samples to run, a faint piano somewhere low in the mix. It's a fantastic if brief piece of music, that I wish had gone on for a lot longer. 'Under the Son' is an unusual title. Can you tell us where that came from?

It's hard to know when to spell things out and when not to. At a general level a title is just a handle to pick something up. To identify it. But I like it when something is a little ambiguous, it makes the mind search for meaning in an interesting way I think. I want there to be a poetic idea. So there's always a number of layers going into titles or lyric. If you want, here is the kind of train of thought for me. It's some kind of pun on "Nothing new under the sun" (Donne) and "the sun shone on the nothing new" (Beckett) but with the "new" wrong spelling on son. The son obviously having a resonance of the son of the father. Of God and of course now G.B. senior. The "under" for me suggests living in the context of power. And this connects with *The Beating of Wings* which again perhaps this is only anecdotally interesting, but that is a reference to Herod at the end of Wilde's Salome. Which I later used as the basis of a chamber Opera. Sun and Wings invoke Icarus and perhaps somewhere I'm talking to myself about my ambition and power. Incidentally David Owen told me that *The Beating of Wings* is classic Freudian dream imagery for sexual anxiety. I always think about wings at the end of 'The Impossible Net', the sound of the reverbs and delays dyeing away. Something has flown the coup. Can I just add a rider to all this. The music isn't expressing any of these things. I think of literary ideas as actually working on a different plane from the musical. Of course they come together in an experience. But that experience is heterogeneous. And we can have this discussion now, in the form of words, about the music, but the music isn't happening. When it is, we're somewhere else. Hopefully in the music.

As we're at this confession thing "a mystery dance" is Elvis Costello.

Am I right in my surmising that 'The Passage' uses musical ideas you first worked on with 'Listening In'? Would you agree that it's a more successful track?

Well they are both very sequenced with lots of rhythmic energy. But 'The Passage' is a very different and more ambitious piece. There is a lot more construction in the harmonic and rhythmic things. 'Listening In' is very very simple. Which is fine. I'm really pleased that you like 'The Passage' over 'Listening In' because it's on a much bigger scale and is harder to grasp perhaps. It's been sitting there for 20 years and not many people have heard it. Glyn Perrin was always saying to me what an interesting piece it was and that something should happen to it.

I think 'Sometimes It Rains' is fantastic! Were there other compositions like this at the time? It has a massive presence and 'weight', seems to have come from a different place to most of your music. I love the total shift in the music when the rhythm track drops out. Or do you simply see it as another remix/ sampling project?

There are a number of pieces from this time that are still unrecorded. It depends what you mean by "like this". When I look at any of the pieces I don't see them as being very similar. There are some pieces that have a similar rhythmic energy. 'Sometimes It Rains' is a studio piece. It's all samples accept for a the piano which is played. Perhaps I should do an album like that. In a way *Time At Rest Devouring Its Secret* (released in 2000 on Source Research) is similar in it approach to the studio. But it sounds very different. It's much more lugubrious and melancholy. Actually that piece was part of a larger CD package that I originally put together called *Blood Sugar*. Hopefully that can see the light of day at some point.

What's it been like hearing all this music again after 15 years or more? How do you feel it works as a body of work?

Well first of all I'm really really grateful to the work that Ian Peel and Pete Garden have put in to get this project out. I really think it's a great package and if you're into the music you can start to see connections and developments now that it's all under one roof.

It's today, June 2005. It would be remiss of me not to point you in the direction of the Andrew Poppy interview published in *Stride* in 2001, or another recent Andrew Poppy CD: *Another Language* is a collaboration

between Propaganda's Claudia Brücken and Andrew Poppy, a CD of song covers released by There (There) earlier in the year.

Andrew, is Another Language *unfinished business between ZTT bands? Or a new project brokered on the back of ZTT's resurrection?*

Over the years I've worked with lots of different people. Choreographers, film makers, theatre directors and bands. So collaboration sits next to my own work as it were. But I try not to just be a servant because I think it leads to a blandness. Or that's what I'm afraid of.

And there is a flow of ideas from one thing to the other. Sometimes when I've worked on other peoples records I've lifted things from say my own string quartet when I thought it was appropriate. But there's not hard and fast rule.

I knew Claudia from the days working at Sarm West Studios. I nearly played some piano on the Act single, 'Snobbery and Decay'. I've got a very early monitor mix on cassette that Steve Lipson gave me. Beautiful. Claudia and I got chatting again about 5 year ago and although we were both busy on other projects we thought it would be nice to do something together.

Talk us through your choice of covers. Favourites or songs that need better versions that the originals?

They are favourite songs. Or songs that are inspiring for some reason. But in all the arrangements I've tried to follow my own path. And Claudia has a very unique voice and personality in popular music. So its up to you to judge.

Masterpiece or temporary diversion? Major statement or musical aside?

Well in some ways it's a very different from writing original music or texts. On *Andrew Poppy on Zang Tumb Tumb* there are some tracks which are like deconstructed songs: 'The Sequence', perhaps 'Listening In' and 'The Amusement'. My chamber opera *Baby Doll* has more song moments than say *Ophelia/Ophelia* which is for one voice. But I've been dealing with the voice since the beginning. Of course it connects to those arranging project in the '80s but it's also a way of trying to talk musically about how what I do connects with songs, and with the recent (last 30 years) pop music. Or maybe it's me trying to find out something about that. The opening of 'Running up that Hill' seems to echo something like Glass's 'Music in Similar Motion'. But again it was an intuitive thing. And works with the image of running. It was also recent songs this might connect with other traditions like German Lieder of Schubert. In a way for me the Schubert song was a starting point. I was playing through the *Winterreise* cycle of 24 songs for voice and piano, every day as part of my practise and realising how amazing they were. Actually 'Die Nebensonnen' (which is song 23 in the Schubert cycle which I arranged for guitar on *Another Language*) was a very late addition to the set. But it really completes the package. I hope there are some thought's that are provoked by the project as well as the sensual pleasure of hearing the songs.

Since your ZTT days there has been lots more music composed and played by Andrew Poppy, though not all of it has made it onto CD. Much of it has been for films and performance; other pieces have been commissioned by both prestigious and unknown ensembles or orchestras.

Andrew, a quick run through, if you please, of your most important post-ZTT releases and performances—or some of them!

The best thing is to visit the website. In the early '90s I made a CD called *Recordings* that is a straight-to-stereo recording at Abbey Road of all acoustic music. Piano, piano and violin, string quartet. It was a way to get back to performance and composition. But you live and die by it. The *Poems and Toccatas* for piano and violin are wonderful performed by Liz Perry and Andrew Ball. But the string quartet performance really needed more work and a better balance. I couldn't afford to do that.

Writing *Horn Horn* (no relation) for Liverpool Philharmonic was a great pleasure. There are six movements and a couple that didn't quite make it to the first and only performance. So there's an album there one day! Jacopo Benci, an Italian video maker, has made a video using the slow movement and that's gone down well at film festivals

I've been developing projects with director/designer/visual artist Julia Bardsley over the years. *Avalanche Thoughts* in New York.

It seems to me that the music world is more fragmented than ever, with a hundred different genres each in its own box. How are you going to overcome that this time round?

I don't think I was ever trying to overcome something. I am interested in how things change and being part of that.

The fragmentation mirrors globalisation don't you think? It's a kind of antidote. Making records is now more like a pre-industrial cottage industry than anything. People doing their own thing and setting up in their own way. I'm not romantic or idealistic about the internet though. But it's some kind of change in the way the world works.

The real problem is the failure of the powers-that-be to understand how culture works. The political left is in some ways worse than the right. Government and big business cream off, trade on what is successful. But it takes the whole network of input to make a rich culture. That's a network that works inside a culture and through time. Stretching back. As you know I used to be interested in opera. But it's a dead duck in terms of being a place to be creative. It's absurd the way these 19th century works, the popular culture of a particular time and place, should be funded in advance of contemporary musical culture. It becomes a self-fulfilling prophecy. It's a vain and pompous flattering of a particular class.

What are you writing and recording at the moment? What can we expect next?

There are always more projects in the cupboard than ever get out in the fresh air. There are two projects that are in go mode. One with a wonderful, Portuguese singer Bernado Devlin. Provisionally called *Let the Handkerchief Fly*. We're hoping to present that in a very original way. It still in development although most of the music is written, I'm also writing something called *Levitation and Fall,* a kind of oratorio for the Estonian National Male Voice Choir conductor Kaspar Putnins. 52 Male voices, mezzo solo, spoken male voice, two percussionists and electronics. The piece will be presented with live sound mix by myself and live vision mix by Julia Bardsley. It's scheduled to première in Tallin in February 2006. Keep an eye on the web site for more details.

It's 2005. There's a beautiful blue and grey box set in a jiffy bag delivered to my door. It's a ZTT box set, featuring most of composer Andrew Poppy's recordings for the company, albums and singles, including an unreleased album. I've been looking forward to this for some time.

Rupert Loydell: *Andrew, I wondered if you'd care to do another interview for* Stride *to tie in with the release of the* Andrew Poppy on Zang Tuum Tumb *box set? Is this release due to '80s nostalgia or long overdue recognition?*

Andrew Poppy: It's pure nostalgia.

Are you going to be a pop star again?

Again? Are you doing something tricksy with the structure here?

[*Stride*, 2005]

Language Is All We Have

An interview with Rupert Loydell

Jeffrey Side: *What got you interested in poetry?*

Rupert Loydell: My Dad reading me *The Waste Land*, seeing Adrian Mitchell read, talking to Brian Louis Pearce, hearing Ted Hughes read *Crow*, finding copies of *Slow Dancer* magazine in an Oxford Street bookshop. Lots of things, many of which I wrote about recently in an essay in *The North*.

How did you get involved in poetry publishing?

Naïve excitement about the possibilities of the small press, having got my first poem published. My mum having a Gestetner duplicator. The poetry group at a hospital where I was working. My friend Graham Palmer who co-edited the first *Stride* magazines.

Has your involvement in poetics informed your painting procedures?

I suspect it's been the other way round, and either way only indirectly.

Do you think non-mainstream poetry has an audience apart from poets, critics and academics?

I'm sure it does, but I'm not sure it matters. Populism doesn't seem a criteria for making or writing, I'm afraid. Maybe a poem will only find one readers—that's OK. Most paintings only end up with one or two viewers once they are placed on somebody's wall.

I think if people understood poetry is first and foremost about language then they would read it. People keep telling them that it's difficult, it's not. It's exhilarating, complex and wonderful.

In what sense can we say that poetry is relevant—or has a purpose?

It's relevant because people write it and we are all people, and because it is written and alive today, in a world we are part of. And because language is how we think and know that world. But I don't expect poetry to be universally relevant—I don't believe anyone can speak for all of us.

It is relevant but I don't think anyone makes poems for everyone. We are too much part of our own individual histories, our gender, our nation, our upbringing, our interests Poetry's purpose? For me to explore how we think and the possibilities of language; for others to share moments and ideas with others; for others to entertain and amuse; for others to preach or instruct; for others to make sound scores or visual artefacts; for others to declare their love or hate; for others to "express themselves". And a million other uses.

Are there limits to experimentation in poetry; if so what are they?

I don't see why there should be, no. That doesn't mean all experiment becomes great writing, but people can attempt what they like with language. I personally have my own limits of what I perceive as poetry, or at least am willing to read; other people go further into experimentation or less further. Authors have their own specific interests and concerns.

Does a poem cease to be "poetic" once the semantic element is excluded and extra-lexical ones such as the use of typographics replace it?

No. It just means a poem is primarily concerned with other parts of poetry rather than the semantic. "Poetic", especially in inverted commas, is a strange word to use, though. It brings to mind flowery thoughts and misty scenes. I'm not keen on poetry that tries to be "poetic". But that's probably not what you meant, is it?

At what point does a visual poem become a visual work of art?

When its maker says so, or when a reader or viewer wants to regard it primarily in visual terms.

Does poetry have to operate semantically to distinguish it from visual art, or is there "something" intrinsic to poetry that inevitability distinguishes it from visual art?

Poetry always works semantically because it uses language as its primary element. What it may do is disrupt expected semantics. I don't believe language can totally be separated from notions of sense or semantics, however abstracted, exploded or cut-up it becomes. (I might allow that the work of people like Bob Cobbing becomes quite difficult to "read" in terms of language, but in the main I feel my point holds—and Bob's work I find easier to view as visual art than poetry, though of course he often regarded his work as art, poetry and sound score!)

Is a poem's semantic element more important than its formal and visual elements?

No. Why should it be? That's like saying is the tone or line more important in art than the colour? It's all up for grabs, and an artist or writer may choose to focus on certain aspects of what they make. The problem comes when anyone says, "this is the only way to write/paint", not otherwise.

When you say that you have to create the world with language, what do you mean?

I mean we think in language. Until we name things, we don't understand or experience the world; all our senses are converted into language. Language is all we have.

In relation to your painting, you have said "Colour, of course, can be as lyrical as any language". What do you mean by this?

I mean I find colour as beautiful and as full of potential as language, and vice versa. And that colour says as much, or as little, as language.

You have said: "Language excites me—you can do so much with it". This suggests that you view language as raw material, aware of its plasticity. Does this view of language grow out of your experience of working with paint?

I'm sure it does have some bearing on it yes, and also I feel that contemporary classical composition and improvised jazz have a mainly subconscious bearing on my current writing. Mainly, however, I have to say that this view of language came about through various friends, colleagues and teachers showing me that plasticity in action, through reading and

Rupert Loydell & Jeffrey Side

critical discussion of poets and poetry new to me at the time, and also through workshops.

You have said that you dislike poetry that is narrative. Do you think the reason that the majority of poetry today is narrative is because of the increase in poetry workshops that tend to teach poetry as a branch of fiction writing?

Well, I'm all for writing workshops if they include critical reading, and separate ideas of enabling and creativity from the end product. We aren't a nation of poetic geniuses or natural poets, and many people should be told their work is not very good nor interesting. It's often not even good therapy. Anybody who has now published one or two poems seems to think they can run a writing workshop! Aspiring poets need to read, read, read, and read some more.

I think most poetry is narrative these days because people don't understand the nature of language, or how poetry can and does work; they're still bound up trying to tell the reader something, not realising how banal and ordinary most human experience is. We don't need any more poems about sunsets, cats or falling in love! I can't believe it when I meet self-declared poets who don't understand syllabics, internal rhyme, half-rhyme, breath pattern, collage, concrete poems, syntactic disruption, prose-poems, etc. etc. and haven't read more than two or three contemporary writers. They often can't even be bothered to get down the library and read some of the wide-ranging anthologies of contemporary poetry, or read something that they find challenging, yet they somehow think their poems are going to be good. People need to understand there is no one correct way to write, there are thousands of processes, and poetic forms available to the poet. I want open-ended poems that explore the language, not something closed, final and declamatory.

Today many poets write without a basic understanding of the historical or literary context they inhabit. It is as if the past 200 years of poetic development had never happened. As a result, they follow only the fashion of the particular poetry workshop they last attended. Is this the reason, perhaps, why so much bland poetry is being written? It seems to me that artists would not find themselves in this position.

I think, as I said above, it's a lack of reading, discussion and critical work—literary criticism and self-criticism. Workshops, whether a local group or a loose affiliation over the internet, can be a godsend and massive support for the writer, but you have to be prepared to actually debate things, to voice an opinion, and to listen to others' criticism. You might also have to accept that whilst you have every right to write poetry, there is no automatic right anyone has to publish it! I'm afraid I think artists of all persuasions and art forms do find themselves in this position. I've long thought local poetry groups, intent on writing end-of-line doggerel and light verse are pretty analogous to the local watercolour groups who simply haven't got any notion of paint beyond using it to make "nice pictures". Each to their own, but let's not pretend it's good art or good poetry.

You have said that you believe myth and allegory is more real than factual truth. Do you think that much of today's poetry is too descriptive and grounded too much in reality?

Some of it, but I think the problem is really that people still try and use myths and stories that many people in today's world simply don't understand or know. Britain is no longer a Christian society, so there's little point in assuming people know about church liturgy or Bible stories. There's little point in assuming everyone has read Shakespeare or Chaucer, or knows the name of Greek gods. Poets need to think about what we currently share in the way of stories and shared experienced. For instance, I think the notion of "the muse" is just ridiculous in the 21st century. My quote actually says I believe in myth and allegory more than factual truth. This was to do with questions of my own beliefs, which isn't quite the same thing. I think people who want to pin everything down and prove this or that happened or exists are in trouble. I've always hovered between faith and doubt, called things into question. I find surety tends towards political and self fascism, the conservative end of things, declamation and bullying. I prefer to be open towards things—this doesn't seem to me to compromise what I personally believe (in).

The various statements you have made on the relationship of the reader to the text I think are very important. For instance, you acknowledge that the reader has a significant role in the creation of a poem's "meaning"; and that poems that are content driven (narrative, confessional, protest, etc.) tend to inhibit this creativity because their didacticism forces the reader into a passive and compliant stance in relation to the text. Whereas poems such as yours, because of their use of collage, assumed voices, asides, associative matter, etc., operate

Rupert Loydell & Jeffrey Side

intertextually, resulting in a wider network of allusion from which the reader
can draw upon to create individual meaning for themselves. If we assume for the
sake of courtesy that mainstream poetry publishers are aware of this approach
to the text and the reader, is their opposition to it based on market forces alone
or sincerely held aesthetic beliefs about the nature of poetry?

I suspect it's to do with both. Neil Astley at Bloodaxe, for instance, seriously
seems to believe in popular poetry—most of which I, and many others,
find pedestrian and dull. But he has sold tens of thousands of copies of
some of his anthologies. However, he has also published the big Prynne
volume, presumably with an eye to both "posterity" and aesthetics but also
the market—that is, he thought he could sell a few hundred and get some
credibility. I do think it sits very uneasily in the Bloodaxe list though! (I
must say that although I find a lot of the Bloodaxe list dull there's also
some great stuff on it, too, especially from the earlier days of the company.)
    Other mainstream publishers don't seem engaged with poetry at all;
it's a kind of token nod to literature, supported by sales of their fiction or
gardening titles. This actually, to my mind, makes it even sillier that their
lists are so mainstream and pedestrian! I'm sure it's basically to do with
saleability or perceived saleability of poetry *per se*, not individual poet's
work. I'd probably argue that mainstream fiction is fairly ordinary in the
main, but of course I'm aware that the influence of William Burroughs,
J.G. Ballard and other experimental writers, often from science fiction
or slipstream genres, have influenced and infiltrated the mainstream and
changed reader's and publisher's perceptions of what can be marketed.

I think you've already answered this question in your previous answer but here
it is anyway: If mainstream publishers' opposition is based on sincerely held
aesthetic beliefs about the nature of poetry how can we account for Carcanet
and Bloodaxe having John Ashbery, Peter Riley, Tom Raworth, Roy Fisher, John
Kinsella, and J.H. Prynne on their poetry lists? Is it a case of these publishers
poaching what others have nurtured to fruition? If so, is this historically
remarkable given the mainstream's adversity to risk taking?

Let me say clearly that in many ways I don't care what the mainstream
publishers publish. Each to their own; good luck to them. What I have
spoken out about in reviews and interviews about publishers and their
lists, and do object to, is if they start believing their own hype about poetry
being "the new rock'n'roll", or some new poet being a genius, when often

it's just more of the same middle of the road tosh. I also don't believe in any trickle-down notion of poetry sales; people who read Simon Armitage or Linda France or whoever don't suddenly rush out and buy Tom Raworth or Robert Creeley books.

I think Simon Thirsk at Bloodaxe is a fantastic marketing man. I heard him speak at a debate at Warwick University on the future of poetry publishing that I was also involved in. But I simply don't believe you can "market" anything or everything—and sell more. I've been involved in Arts Council initiatives where they've spent thousands on promotions and launches and we've sold very few copies of the titles involved as a result. Word of mouth and peer review seems to me to always work better in the long run. As does getting a really huge grant, of course!

I actually think Bloodaxe and many other publishers are using an old business model—trying to flood the market with books they've already printed, making lots of noise about individual or groups of titles whenever possible, and seeing what happens. Bloodaxe got lucky very early on, and followed-through brilliantly, with Ken Smith and Irina Ratushinskaya, but they are still doing the same kind of thing. Since the book trade has changed immeasurably I think it's a problem. The way ahead for the small publisher is print-on-demand and direct sales. As I see it, the two most successful poetry lists at the moment are Salt and Shearsman, both producing fantastic amounts of brilliant poetry in good-looking volumes, with low overheads, great websites and lots of sales. We're somewhere in-between at the moment: Stride hasn't gone over to "true" print-on-demand, but we are doing very short runs/reprints on demand!

Yes, there's an element of poaching going on, but there always has been and will be in the arts. It's only like an indie band signing to a major label, but of course without the big contract fee! I don't think you can suggest Ashbery and such have been poached though—strikes me as more to do with an overdue selection from unobtainable small press volumes (Raworth, Prynne, Kinsella), foreign rights (Ashbery), or in Roy Fisher's case picking up the mess that Oxford left behind. Obviously there's an element of the moment being right—for instance, Tom Raworth and J.H. Prynne are only two of a number of poets being re-assessed in this way with the publication of big Selecteds or Collecteds. (Others include John James, Allen Fisher and Lee Harwood).

You are a supporter of poetry that is difficult because it discloses more of itself with each new reading. You believe that if people read widely and had an understanding of how poetry worked then the issue of difficulty in poetry would

Rupert Loydell & Jeffrey Side

be irrelevant. Do you think this ignorance of how poetry works is particular to British readers, and if so is there an explanation for it?

Actually, I like many sorts of poetry. Much of the poetry that is perceived as "difficult" isn't, it simply doesn't involve linear narratives, self-confession, extended metaphor or epiphanic endings! I used to think this ignorance was particular to Britain, but now I'm not so sure. From over here American poetry seems much more exciting than what's on offer here, but my American friends complain how lacklustre publishers' lists are over there, how cliquey etc—all the same complaints as usual!

I think the British are lazy as a nation: we don't like having to learn things or find out for ourselves. We don't speak foreign languages very well, we expect people to speak our language; we like pictures of pretty things, not art; we like poems which tell a story and have obvious rhymes in. I actually like finding out things for myself, wondering what something might mean rather than being told. As a nation, we don't really seem to have absorbed Modernism yet, do we? Let alone Postmodernism! I do feel in general terms that poets in America took on board Pound and learnt from him, whereas we got Eliot, retreating back into conservatism and declamation. We don't even understand him, do we? We prefer to try and annotate *The Waste Land* for A Level than start thinking about language and fragmentation, the music of the poem.

If a poet hasn't read, have some knowledge of, or simply isn't aware of (off the top of my head) the Beats, Dada and Surrealism, the Objectivists, Eliot, Pound, Olson, Duncan, the New York School, Black Mountain College, L=A=N=G=U=A=G=E poets, Bunting, concrete poetry, the Liverpool poets, Auden, Berryman, MacNeice, William Carlos Williams, Ted Hughes, then they're in trouble. I haven't even touched on works in translation or from non-Western cultures. If they aren't reading contemporary poetry then they're in trouble. If they aren't reading poetics then they're in trouble. If they can't shape language in any other way than prioritising content then they are in trouble.

I want people to be excited by poetry. It's not that I like or would proscribe difficult poetry—it's that language is fantastic stuff. If a poet isn't excited and surprised by language then they may as well forget it. And a lot of what comes through my door for review or submission is neither exciting nor surprising.

[*The Argotist Online*, 2005]

Time and Place

An Interview with Iain Sinclair

RUPERT LOYDELL: *There seems to me a certain amount of editorial distancing yourself involved in* Conductors of Chaos: *you rather disingenuously claim that the anthology almost put itself together. Do you not feel part of this kind of poetry? Or is it just a defensive move?*

IAIN SINCLAIR: *Conductors of Chaos* is dust. It was published as dust. The commissioner of the project, a man I'd met through my activities as a used book-dealer (he assembled junkheaps of Booker shortlists and the like), wanted me to edit an anthology of pulp crime writing. The obvious move was to trade sideways into pre-pulped poetry.

The introduction was strategic, designed to infuriate the deadbeat verse-police who operate in the corners of broadsheets (it had the bonus of also infuriating many of the small-press essayists). Otherwise, quite simply, the anthology would have been unreviewed. Scorn was the best we could hope for, an argument. The meat of the book was the poetry. Much of which I admire, some of which I love. Choices were again strategic: I thought that this sort of public manifestation required poets who were prepared to perform. My sympathies are still—always were, always will be—with this writing. I think, from the mid-Sixties, most of what is worth putting on paper comes from poets (and the prose-visionaries associated with Moorcock's *New Worlds* stable). Some of whom are still marching. It's a period now of elegiac gatherings-up, the bolting together of collections by presses like Shearsman, Reality Studios, Etruscan Books and the ubiquitous (but covertly virtual) Salt. (All my books, one way or another, pay their dues to that landscape.)

It could be argued that the likes of Salt and Shearsman both seem to have concluded the publishing project you started with your Paladin anthologies, namely a remapping of British 20th Century poetry. Do you think we will now see the likes of Tom Raworth, Allen Fisher and Lee Harwood take their rightful places in a poetic/literary (alternative?) canon alongside David Jones, Basil Bunting and W.S. Graham? Or is the postmodern world so fractured that any kind of critical agreement is no longer possible, or perhaps even desirable?

It's a fine thing that blocks of Raworth, Harwood, Prynne, Griffiths, John James, Wendy Mulford are becoming, if you search hard enough, available. I don't believe this impacts on the flabby centre of things: the compulsory amnesia, the fog of spite, vanity and self-preservation. We have, after all, the most successful Poet Laureate there has ever been, a customised New Labour figure: visible, camera-friendly, on the move—and positioned as far as it is possible to be from the heart of the matter, the old heat.

There will be minor political shifts in the poetry mapping, strange alliances (Mao and Mandelson). By unimagined accidents, Prynne's "difficulty" will be manoeuvred alongside Larkin's availability as a two-minute radio feature. (If you go back far enough, deep enough into the vaults, you'll find Prynne reading and discussing his work on the old Third Programme, at the time of the publication of his first book.)

So: poets do take their place in the canon of the academically respectable (funded research, readings, forms to fill), but not in the Ghost World of goldfish memory (last night's TV is smoke you can try to trap in a bottle). David Jones and Basil Bunting have no visibility here either and W.S. Graham's survival relies on the sponsorship of such as Harold Pinter.

None of this matters. What lasts, lasts. The doing is more important than the selling. Obviously, yes, the energy of that moment, the so-called "British Poetry Revival" (or whatever), will become a brand, a franchise, a local industry. Mimeo to mausoleum in forty years.

Why do you think poetry has become so fractured and ignored? Are you someone who believes poetry ever was, or ever could be, populist, or has it always been a minority interest?

Poetry is intense. It takes time, concentration, intelligence: qualities that are not readily available. The payback is not instant. Populism is something else—and frequently involved with performance, staying on the road, like those Archie Rice vampire-figures who have been doing the festivals since the Second War (when the major schism occurred: the mask of English irony muzzled continental and transatlantic influences). This was mostly fear and careerism, but it worked.

How do you differentiate between your prose, which at times is very poetic, and your poetry? How do you write your poems—are they processual, improvised, heavily edited and reworked, collaged?

I write prose, now, to make a living: it's a late profession. I know there are people looking over my shoulder. I use techniques from subterranean years of small-press poetry composition and publishing—and the reading of other poets—to give the thing its bite (if any). But I'm aware that I have to shape material towards a potential audience (however small). My kind of fiction exists in the place where poetry used to be (in the period 1965-1975): a few hundred readers, a few unpublic readings. The books of mine which perform best, though the content is much the same, are the ones that appear in "Travel" sections. You have to be able to lay the pitch down in a single sentence: "I walk around the M25."

Meanwhile, poetry—that spasm, the notebook—is freed up as an hermetic (largely unpublished) activity. I suppose a mad hobby, reflex compulsion. I've been assembling a collection, mostly written on the South Coast, called *Buried at Sea*. With the prose, I have to know pretty much what I'm doing. The other stuff, as with our dialogue between blind machines, comes off the top of my head: uncensored, very fast (the poems will be worked over before they reach daylight). I fill a notebook with tight scribble and then, if I can sneak a day or two, over Christmas or whenever, I make copies. See what I've got.

In an ideal world, I'd like to take time out to work through the files: much, much more is unpublished than published (rightly so).

The linguistically experimental work in Conductors *seems a long way away from the work of Allen Ginsberg and the beats, which your poetry seems to have originally been influenced and inspired by. Could you talk about how your poetry has developed?*

I would say that what has happened in my life, the kind of other writing I do, has fixed the poetry. It is now a very strange beast, fiercely inelegant, awkward and unconcerned with shape and structure. I grew up with Beat writing (especially Burroughs and Kerouac) but the major poetic influence would have been Olson, Black Mountain and the tradition that takes in Ed Dorn, J.H. Prynne and John Wieners. I don't know who would relate to what

I am now doing: I have been reading Celan, Brian Catling, Bob Dylan's *Chronicles* and Anthony Mellors' book on 'Late Modernist Poetics from Pound to Prynne'. What I miss, really, is the making of the book as an object: the old vanity of self-publication, getting it done, clean, when and how you fancied. Using images, inserts. Shipping the booklets out or taking them over to Compendium in Camden Town. Making swaps. Gossip with Mike Hart. Putting the business in other hands is the first mistake, from which all problems accrue. It was fine when publishers were themselves poets. That is a climate to be reclaimed, perhaps by the internet (though not by me).

My poetry was one thing, mixing documentation and lyric, up to the publication of *Lud Heat* and *Suicide Bridge*. At which point, I felt, the game was over. I couldn't push further in that direction. The novel *White Chappell, Scarlet Tracings* was the final lurch in that direction: it belonged in the Seventies, not the Eighties.

I then went on the road as a book-dealer, poetry was resolutely occasional, booklets were published and given away. But I feel, presently, that I'd like to put something together, a more substantial sequence: a shift to marine light. (Hastings feels so much like old Hackney: crime as nostalgia.)

William Blake?

I've said too much about Blake. He is one of the inspirations for the sturdy independence (at the edge of mania) that I've been describing: the work-life. His mapping of London is still the most useful to me. I visit the place where he isn't buried, the memorial slab in Bunhill Fields, often. And relish the triangulation with Bunyan and Defoe. Non-conformity is the only conformity worth having.

And how did film come into it? You were at film school in London, yes? Were you there as a writer for films or as a filmmaker per se?

I began as a film-maker, actually shooting film, hands-on: 8mm and 16mm. I went to the film school in Brixton and got my first taste of London life. (I was writing poetry. I never liked, and still don't, writing film scripts. A few doodles on a sheet of paper, a few drawings and off.) The keeping of a film diary (1969-1975), influenced by such as Stan Brakhage, went in parallel with the publications from Albion Village Press: versions of lives and places (lyric and documentary again). A late collaboration with Chris Petit (and digital technology) has opened up new (old) possibilities: film as essay. The film version of the M25 book, *London Orbital*, was very useful to me, as research and as a "poetic" response to material worked over for public consumption. Speedier editing processes allow us the freedom that was previously available only to writers in their solitude. Using film as a front, I was able to meet and interview writers like J.G. Ballard, Francis Stuart, Derek Raymond. It was an excuse to visit David Gascoyne on the Isle of Wight: a few moments of tea-party, in shimmering afternoon light, shot for a poetry reading at the Albert Hall.

I am talking to Chris, at the moment, about ways of getting back to making films outside the commissioning process (which is silted up, loss of nerve, obsession with celebrity—all the old commissioning editors have now stuck themselves in front of the cameras, doing the baby talk, making everything sound like Blue Peter).

You delight in forgotten authors and hidden narratives. Do you hunt out the unknown and obscure, or do you simply come across them? Presumably when you were book dealing there were things that caught your eye?

I take great delight in the apparently forgotten. As Ed Dorn said, "just because you don't see something, it doesn't mean that it's not there." I'm editing a fat book for Hamish Hamilton called *London: City of Disappearances*. An ironic concept: producing the mounds to prove that they no longer exist. Along with vanished buildings, books, people, there are accounts written by the re-forgotten themselves. One unfashionable writer will often lead us to another. Certain names, promoted from time to time, make up a spectral establishment: Patrick Hamilton, Gerald Kersh, Jean Rhys, J. Maclaren-Ross, W. Pett Ridge, Arthur Morrison, Mary Butts. I'm happy that I have been able, at one level, to make the *Disappearances* book into a sequel to *Conductors of Chaos*. Contributors include: Jeff Nuttall, Lee Harwood, Tom Raworth, Bill Griffiths, Allen Fisher, John Seed, Brian Catling, Vahni Capildeo, Alexis Lykiard, Paul Buck, Stewart Home, Ben Watson, Tony Rudolf, John Welch. Alongside: Marina Warner, J.G. Ballard, Michael Moorcock, Derek Raymond, Jim Sallis, Will Self, Alan Moore, Sarah Wise, Rachel Lichtenstein, Tibor Fischer—and the film-makers, Patrick Keiller, Andrew Kötting, Chris Petit.

Just as I've suggested you distanced yourself as editor of the Conductors of Chaos *anthology, I feel you do the same kind of thing with some of the more occult themes in your books. The reader is never sure whether you dismiss or champion the power lines and dark forces you suggest exist as part of "place".*

Could I ask you what you actually believe—are these fictions or deeply felt ideas?

About the occulted elements of the books. Of course, a slippery ambiguity of approach is the preferred method. Belief shifts. It is never fixed. Theories are road tested. What is written is what is felt, at that instant. Fiction operates with improvised versions of an unanchored self. I'm drawn towards all kinds of curious theories, but I'm not going to make a career out of preaching them (elective Mormonism, industrial weirdness). Somehow the darker pitches, once you give them house-room, and present them with a particular force, evolve into mass hysteria. Always a slot, as Dan Brown knows, for another good conspiracy. If you want fame and fortune go for Xerox occultism. The shamanism of intent, a much harder path, is more appealing.

You've left London now, I believe, but for years it has been both the theme and setting for the majority of your fiction and non-fiction. Could you talk about what London has meant to you, how it differs from other metropolises or the rural?

I haven't left London. I'm in the place where I've been since 1969. I do spent time, a few weekends, the odd snatched week, on the South Coast—but, for the most part, my days are fixed in the old routine. Matters became confused when I published a novel, *Dining on Stones*, that made play with the shifts between fiction and documentation, between East London (the A13 corridor) and a coastal exile. The really strange moment came when, out of nowhere, I met a Dublin poet I hadn't seen in forty years, on the sea-front in St Leonards. I gave him the book. He rang me, in deep shock. It was his story, he said. The right building, the lost books and wives, the underworld connections. I seem to have transcribed this man's memoirs, without having the faintest notion that he'd moved to the coast—or having thought about at all him since I left Dublin (except when I noticed his name, from time to time, on the credits of cop shows like *The Sweeney*). My thesis, about fictions existing independently of their supposed authors—a poetry of place (Henry James, Conrad, Ford, Stephen Crane remaking English prose)—was proved by the collision with another writer. And the feeling that my book, and my very existence on the coast, might be no more than shadows of a more real banishment.

Although London has been your main theme it has been the detail and often everyday, even mundane, people and parts of the city that you use to assemble your books. Why is the everyday so important to you: the local café, the local boozer, the push and shove of market day, the abandoned mental asylum. Is it the sense of history in the making? The accumulation of individuals that somehow builds up into some larger whole?

And how does that then link to the bigger facts and events you choose to engage with? Why is the M25 important to London? To you? Why does the Thames seduce you so? Why does the East End demand to be documented in the manner you choose—a mix of mythology, occult and documentary?

I've banged on about place, city, edge lands, so often and in so many interviews, that I'll refer anyone interested to the books. A hobbled trilogy worries at everything I have to say on the subject: *Lights Out for the Territory* (centre, labyrinth, walking), *London Orbital* (the fringe, the limping future uncovered from a reading of 19th-century speculative fiction), & published in September—*Edge of the Orison: In the Traces of John Clare's 'Journey out of Essex'*—which draws the distance of the walk around the M25 out into the English countryside (nobody at home). I re-walk Clare's escape from Epping Forest to Werrington (north of Peterborough) and contemplate the blight of coming motorway-corridor estates (Stansted to Cambridge to Peterborough). Flying, dreaming, walking, drowning. Another period, 1821-30, when the Romantic poetry franchise went out of fashion. Clare plunged from popular success (first book syndrome, great pitch: Peasant Poet), to obscurity and madness. Handy metaphors.

Can you surmise what happened in the 1990s' publishing world that allowed the author Iain Sinclair to produce several basically avant-garde fictions and experimental documentary titles and have them successfully mass-marketed and sold? Although the word psycho-geography got bandied about and a few writers seemed to have had books out in the wake of your titles, you and your work seem to still pretty much stand alone. Is that window of opportunity as wide open for you as it has been or is it starting to close again?

I see the changes in publishing, as in the music industry—that is the possibilities of cheap production and dissemination of writing and music—as a fantastic opportunity, but the major publishing houses still cling to concepts of huge investment and mass marketing. Do you think print-on-demand publishing and the internet will finally be accepted and change mainstream publishing?

I think the climate has changed, colder in some spots, meltdown in others. The slippage from the small-press world (where such as Peter Ackroyd got their start) won't happen again. "Literary fiction" has lost its marketing niche: speed has increased, front-of-house display to smoky oven in nanoseconds. What publishers are looking for is the photogenic, one-idea pitch, the first novel. Novelty as a form of celebrity: look good, look wild-but-safe. Have a story. The author is being sold as much as the property.

The answer is, as always, to ignore the system and stake out your own turf. Through internet publishing, events, private circulation. Don't accept the fruit-fly demands of the chains: books don't lose value because they fail to shift thousands of units in the first week.

It's bleak, but it always was. Time and place contrive the voices that time and place require.

[*The Argotist Online*, 2005]

No Public Language

AN INTERVIEW WITH KEN EDWARDS

RUPERT LOYDELL: *Your book is called* No Public Language. *Is this a denial of the possibility of us all sharing a language, or a declaration that your book is private?*

KEN EDWARDS: Not at all! The title comes from a poem in *Intensive Care* (one of the constituent books of the collection): "No public language that is / fit for such a time". It was a heartfelt response to events, as I recall. I worry that the title comes across as overly negative, but my desperate hope has always been to find a public language to share. It's just that it's not as easy as you'd think. I certainly don't believe in private languages anyway.

There's a clear critique of capitalism and media in your work, which we also find in the work of, for example, Tony Lopez and Robert Sheppard, both writers you have been associated with. Is this a generation thing? Were you the first generation that were influenced by poststructuralism and media/critical theory?

If you find such a critique it's probably there. But it isn't what drives my writing. I don't set out to critique late capitalism, or whatever; but I certainly find much of the public realm inimical to the work of the imagination, and such frustrations are doubtless made clear. I can't speak for Tony or Robert, but my writing is most definitely not driven by poststructuralism or media/critical theory. In fact, I often feel hostile to it, and I don't think I'm well read in it. I try to read philosophy, but I haven't even made much inroad into Derrida, for example.

How does the notion of the political square with experimental writing? Aren't you dealing with a small audience who probably share your views?

I'm far less likely than I once was to equate radical form with radical (left-wing) politics. If you were to put together those who are into formally radical poetry and those into radical left-wing politics, the overlapping group would certainly be tiny.

Music is clearly important to your work. Is it an inspiration or a resource? If it's the case, can you talk about the relationship between the idea of dub (or the remix) and textual collage?

Music of all kinds has always been an inspiration. I think what you're referring to is some of the writing I was doing in the 1980s, around the era of my book *Drumming & Poems*, which deliberately used the metaphor of dub/remix to challenge the notion of a fixed composition.

I didn't know you were a composer. Is your music processual or procedural? At all related to your writing? Do you write librettos or songs?

I wouldn't make too many claims for myself as a composer. I started composing about 12 years ago, out of frustration that I wasn't a good enough musician to play the kind of music I wanted. Although I did write and perform songs a bit in my 20s. As I write, a piece of mine is about to be performed at the new Brighton library by COMA, a group comprising amateur and professional musicians. It takes the musical material of a song I wrote a few years ago, fragments it and distributes it among four ensembles who play simultaneously while situated at different points in the performance space. I've also recently written incidental music for a poem by Fanny Howe, which has been published/recorded by Artery Editions. And I've written the text for a piece composed by John Tilbury, of AMM fame, so that's a case of the writing and music coming together. I hope that will be out on CD one day. Recently, I've been taking up the guitar again, and Elaine persuaded me the other evening to play and sing in an open session at one of our local pubs in Hastings Old Town. I was terrified!

Much of your work has dealt with the city, and you state that moving away from London has instigated a move toward prose writing. Could you talk about that?

I lived in London for 35 years, and the city has certainly left its mark on my writing. Moving away from London to Hastings, where I now live, did not "instigate a move towards prose writing" but did coincide with a move *back* to prose, which is where I started. In the 1970s I was mostly writing short stories that sometimes experimented with form and language; I had some publishing success, but was unable to progress in the direction I wanted to, through inexperience and lack of peer support, I suppose. I thought what the poets were doing was so much more interesting! Also poetry enabled me to break up and complicate my texts and procedures, and to break easy habits, which is what I wanted to do. I've always thought of myself as a "writer" rather than a "poet". As for the inspiration of the city, the main prose piece I've written in the past two years, 'Nostalgia for Unknown Cities', very much bears upon that, and the longest section is an immense collage of sentences generated in and by the experience of London. Anyway, it could be seen as poetry by other means. As is my novel *Futures* by the way.

Where do you place your writing? Who are your peers and predecessors? What is your literary lineage?

Goodness, what a question! Predecessors: the prose rhythms of Beckett, the imagery of Kafka and much science-fiction, the fizz of the New York school of poets, and hey, what about the films of Hitchcock, Buñuel, Michael Powell, the music of Bartók, Stravinsky, John Coltrane, Captain Beefheart, the Beatles… As for peers, there are far too many to mention, and it would be invidious to mention only some.

Was the decision to exclude Good Science *from the book simply because it remains in print? I have to confess I think it's a major absence from the Selected Poems!*

Yes. Anyone who wants it can still buy that book. Given that there was only a limited number of pages available for the *Selected Poems*, it seemed therefore a waste to include it at the expense of stuff that's out of print.

[*Stride*, 2006]

Poetic Revolution

ROBERT SHEPPARD'S *THE EDUCATION OF DESIRE*
& KEN EDWARDS' *GOOD SCIENCE*

Both Ken Edwards and Robert Sheppard have written in *fragmente* magazine about discovering American Language poetries. In his essay, 'The Remake', Edwards [1990, p57] talks about how "it rapidly became apparent that [t]here was a new excitement in American poetry, and that ... this poetic revolution had at its fulcrum a radical revaluation of what language is, and the relationship of language to poetry." He goes on [pp57-58] to suggest that "'Making the familiar strange' has ever been one of Modernism's methods and 'the familiar' in this case ... is in fact language, that community of meaning-generation we take for granted most of the time." Sheppard meanwhile, a few pages later, in 'Recognition and Discovery in the 1980's' [Sheppard, 1990, p60] writes about his poetry already "embrac[ing] modernist defamiliarisation and self-consciousness" before discovering "the New American Poets". He wanted [p 60] to

> extend the inherited paradigms of "poetry" ... by delaying a reader's process of naturalization, by using new forms of poetic artifice and formalist techniques to defamiliarise the dominant reality principle, in order to operate a critique of it; and that it should use indeterminacy and discontinuity as major devices of this politics of form, which was implicitly utopian. The reader thus could become an active co-producer of the text...

As well as a creative impetus to write anew, there is a political edge to this poetry. Douglas Messerli [1984, p142], one of the main publishers of the Language Poets, with his Sun & Moon Press, says in an interview in *Gargoyle* magazine:

> For me... language is just *everything*. It is the way—the only way—we have of making reality, the act others describe as "comprehending experience". But, for me, it is truly a "making". Every day every moment we *speak* and, through language, *think* the world into existence.
>   Therefore, it's of the utmost experience that a few of us ...

spend some time contemplating, playing with, challenging, and delighting the ways in which the society uses it.

Hopefully, we can affect a few people, who can ... affect two more, who can affect two more and so on... and so on... until we have the whole country re-evaluating, listening to, and reinventing language—not as an intellectual exercise, but as a matter of life and death...

Robert Sheppard considers the same area of concern in his essay 'The Education of Desire', originally written as a hand-out sheet for A-Level English students [Sheppard, 1983] but later incorporated into both his chapbook of poetics, *net/(k)not - work(s)* [Sheppard, 1993] and his book of critical writing, *Far Language* [Sheppard, 1999]. In it he suggests [1999, p28] that "a lot of poetry today will look like adverts" and that "What once belonged to poetry has been stolen". Although "some poets don't worry about this", he declares that "it is impossible to write revolutionary poetry like this", so that "the writer who wants to do something different has to write in new ways". This, he says, will mean:

The poetry may seem strange. It may be difficult to understand. There may seem to be bits of it missing. There may be problems in putting all its parts together; things may not seem to follow on. It may be difficult to see who's speaking. It may seem as though there should be a story, but there isn't.

He adds:

I'm talking about difficulties that stop the process of reading, or upset your reading habits.

Having considered what the writer must do, should they wish to write revolutionary poetry, he goes on [p29] to consider what the *reader* has to do, because "most of the poetry I am thinking of is not easy to read. You can't consume it one go". Not only does this make "the reader work harder", it also "does something else too: it makes the reader's work as important as that of the writer". In fact Sheppard goes to far as to say that:

It is the reader who makes the poem—or rather: each individual has to make the poem, to complete it, for his or herself.

The reader is no longer a passive consumer.

He then goes on to link this new writing with the idea of 'Making a New World', where "the writer will rearrange everything so that out of the bits and pieces of this world, he or she will make a new world", which, "is a way of criticising the way things are" in the real world. This way of writing will, he suggests [pp 29-30], "be a little bit revolutionary, although it will never tell you *how* things might change", it is only "a way of criticising the way things are".

He also says [p30] that although "linked to the notion of a more active reader" that he "think[s] it can ... be a delightful thing to be allowed as much freedom as the writer, to read creatively, to fill in gaps, to decide who is speaking, etc." And he reassures, saying that, unlike advertising, romantic fiction, pornography and most poems:

> The new poetry doesn't fulfil you. It leaves you with still a lot of thinking to be done. There will always be more and more to think about.   [...]
> It might make you confused, mixed up. But that's all right. When you're trying to understand something difficulty you get confused for a bit.

This idea of revolutionary poetry means there is an onus on the writer to find new ways and processes to write and use language. As the 'Preface' to *Good Science*, Ken Edwards [1992, pp1-3] offers "A note to the reader on some self-imposed procedures in the making of this book, their use, and an indication of some possible responses". In a review of *Good Science*, Robert Sheppard [1994, p99] suggests that this 'Preface' "amounts almost to a manifesto of the linguistically innovative poetries of this country". The instructions include [Edwards, 1992, pp1-2]:

> See clearly with clear eyes. Be strong, harmonic and geological. ... Hint at a place beyond speech. Alternately speak, and indicate the silence beyond speech. ... Create something modern and intrinsic, sensitive and strong. Treat words with the contempt they deserve. ... Learn everything you can, and forget everything you have learnt ... Replace experience with language.

Many of the poems contained in *Good Science* read as fractured and assembled texts with no linear meaning, simply a gathering of events and experiences. In the title poem [pp7-8], the narrator "state[s his] case on the basis of need" whilst "You", an unnamed protagonist, "shoot[s] it down on the basis of want". The gathering of knowledge:

> This week has given me a new grasp of particle physics
> You see how the glands in your throat do swell

exterior events, whether observed first-hand or reported to the author [p7]:

> The Dow is up the unit starts to break down
> …
> A light plane trails red fly north-west

and personal occurrence [p7]:

> My legs start to shake uncontrollably

lead only to the strange observation [p8] that

> The elephant house is blinded with plywood.
> It contains the ghost that language doesn't need

Knowledge, it seems, is not always obtainable [p8]:

> After a heavy day the book was no more than adequately clear
> [...]
> There's no objective way of measuring space

and only leads to a state where

> Extended intervals are occurring

and the observation that

> The big building is full of really crazy people

Somehow the "you" is better at dealing with the information that the poet has gathered. Whilst the narrator suggests, in the penultimate line [p8], that

You dovetail neatly into the above stuff

the narrator himself is reduced to confusion as the poem ends:

I wake up I open the refrigerator I don't know where I am

The narrator of these poems is suffering from an overload of event and information; he appears lost and confused as he tries to make sense of the world of consumerism and knowledge. At the end of 'Lashed to the Mast' [p30] he suggests this information is "the white noise / of a no-signal screen…", yet continues with:

were I to reach to switch
that off
I'd switch the darkness on

If he tried to disengage from the information around him, he will only end up in the dark (although if he is bewildered and doesn't understand then he is "in the dark" anyway!). He must learn a new way of seeing the world around him, must map and then navigate through the facts and figures which he struggles to keep up with.

One way of doing this is to reconsider history, refusing to regard it as "set in stone" or absolute. Edwards hints at the fictional nature [the "neverness"] of fact in 'After a Season the Syntax Falls' [pp51-56] which ends by combining melancholy with a big statement [p56]:

Through your half-window
a little blues must fall
a scent of history trembling
at the wrists of never

He also jokily observes in 'And 'Mid This Tumult' [p62] that the science of the book's title is in flux and cannot be known too; in fact it is dangerous as well as "amazing":

That's technology for you
Nothing is safe any more it's amazing.

Everything, it seems, is in flux. In 'After A Season the Syntax Falls' [pp51-

56], one of the key poems in the book, "what was a factory or church / becomes a theme park" and "what was a hospital becomes / a hologram of commerce" [p53]. Even the business world of today seems unreal:

> A bank of 20 screens
>> & a glaze of money on each one
>> you feel that it all must have
>> happened a long time ago

The present seems like history, and history is not to be regarded as truth. Meanwhile, "white noise" is used to filter out the background noise of contemporary life, the sounds of the world around us [p52]:

> They feed white noise in
>> to make believe it's quiet

The darkness Edwards suggests is the only alternative to the white noise also reappears [p52], as the poet asks in bewilderment where is he?

> What is this place? a surplus value
>> of meaning? the way a shadow
>> falls, drains into poetry, the way
>> a shadow falls the way a shadow falls

Later, in 'New Word Order' [pp63-64], the title itself a pun on the "new world order" around him, he wittily discusses the "game" of poetry that the narrator is engaged in, managing to be both funny and serious at the same time:

> ...it's a game
> Where facetiousness
> And seriousness are inseparable; where
> The jocular and the intimate form a badinage
> Which conceals, reveals for a moment,
> Then conceals again. On the other hand
> Things are more like they are now
> Than they ever were before.
> Things is things, and words is words; the game *is* a game,
> A free lunch *is* a free lunch,

It is no longer a metaphor, a penis *is* a penis, a cigar
Is a cigar

Sometimes, of course, the overload can prove too much and the poet goes missing [p66]:

I'm sorry there is no-one here to answer your call but if
you'd like to leave a message I'll get back to you.

This allows the narrator to step back from the chaos he has previously conjured up, and wonder:

Was there a time, then, when the word
And the action, word & thing
Coalesced, when the shape of it
Was not all that there was…

He blames consumerism and capitalism, for [p69]

This has been made possible by our sponsors…

In the closing section of the poem [pp69-71] he turns to the domestic, returning to the "you" he has made:

And then there was you. No I hadn't forgotten

But she is not innocent either, for she

…built a temple of money
Where a house of love should stand

in the same way that, where "the homes of the privileged" are, "Lawns & golf courses" have sprung up instead of wilderness.

The poet [p71] goes on to reveal that even the personal and domestic is only partially "true":

Even though I invent the story of you, though I put in
the detail, the answering machine, though I make it into
a love story, as incandescent as a narrative without an

ending can be, still your mouth says mutely that I have
not reached you.

His love story has failed, and consumerism and development are rampant
[p70]:

...the world's grown old. It has become a habit.

and the poem ends with further instructions that verge on defeatist:

Make love, & put it right,
And if you can't make love
Make war, & put it right.

along with a vague non-syntactical final line of command, both echoing
the 'Preface' poem and returning to his theme of dark & light:

But never send to know for whom the lights change

Although this would seem a cause for despair, it is countered by the
author's recognition, a kind of resigned optimism, at the start of the poem
[p63] that the multi-layered world around him, full of contradiction and
confusion, can offer endless possibilities for revolutionary poetry as much
as despair and overload:

When all is said & done, then
There is everything still to say & do;

WORKS CITED

Edwards, K., (1990), 'Language: The Remake' in *fragmente* 2, pp57-60, Durham: *fragmente*.
Edwards, K., (1992), *Good Science*, New York: Roof Books.
Messerli, D., (1984), 'Language in Action: An Interview with Douglas Messerli' in *Gargoyle*
    24, pp136-148, Washington DC: Paycock Press.
Sheppard, R., (1983), *The Education of Desire*, London: Ship of Fools.
Sheppard, R., (1990), 'Recognition and Discovery in the 1980s' in *fragmente* 2, pp60-61,
    Durham: *fragmente*.
Sheppard, R., (1993), *net/(k)not - work(s)*, London: Ship of Fools.
Sheppard, R., (1994), 'Little Stars and Straw Beasts' (including review of *Good Science*) in
    Angel Exhaust Ten: Screed Heid, pp99-100, Cambridge: *Angel Exhaust*.
Sheppard, R., (1999), *Far Language: poetics and linguistically innovative poetry 1978-1997*,
    Exeter: Stride.

[*Stride*, 2006]

An Interview with Greg Bottoms

RUPERT LOYDELL: *I came across your writing in the first instance because I asked for a review copy of* The Colorful Apocalypse, *your recent book about outsider art. I was pleasantly surprised—though surprised I was—that the book wasn't what I expected. Neither academic tome nor coffee table picture book, you offer a very individual yet also informative and knowledgeable exploration of naive art as the result of religious compulsion. Was the book always going to be written in the way it was? How did you first get interested in outsider art, and was it always linked in your mind to religion?*

GREG BOTTOMS: I let the material dictate the form, or I followed what seemed to be the story and figured out the best way to deal with it, which is what I always do, I suppose. I once called it a "lyric documentary"—a series of narrative scenes, essayistic reflections, autobiographical elements when seemingly relevant, and cultural reportage and criticism all hopefully in the service of the larger story, which is to say the story according to little old me. I knew it would be a personal travel narrative. This is partly because I find an overt subjectivity, an "I" as the teller/maker, to be the most reasonable and intellectually solid ground to stand on, particularly if we conceive of "objectivity" as an impossibility, though of course the criticisms of this "I" spilling over into self-absorption or self-aggrandizement can have a point, so the "I" thing is tricky. I also knew, before I wrote a word, the book would be driven by questions and ideas about obsession, the ordering aspects of creativity, superstitious modes of thinking as ways toward self-definition when rational modes lead toward bleak or dark findings, and some questions about "madness" and "ecstasy"—what they are, how we might define them and how those definitions change as contexts and sensibilities and purposes change. I knew this because no matter what I write about I seem to often end up there. "Writing reveals your obsessions," wrote Milan Kundera in *The Art of the Novel*. Does it ever.

I got particularly interested in outsider art as a category and an idea when I was writing the book about my brother's schizophrenia, *Angelhead*. I came across Hanz Prinzhorn's *Artistry of the Mentally Ill*, and many of the artists in the book exhibited religious obsessions and delusions just as my brother had, almost exactly at times as my brother had. They had a "mission" in a grand narrative of God, of good and evil, and they became so devoted to the importance of this mission that they became unable to function in mainstream society. Religious delusion is undoubtedly the most typical kind of delusion in psychosis, and I recently saw a statistic that said that over 50% of people suffering from psychosis do not believe they are suffering from psychosis—they've figured it out and everybody else is wrong. And John Locke, long ago, suggested that religion itself, particularly extreme forms, could be seen as "folly," which would translate to madness or psychosis. I'm not saying that that's how I see it, only that this convergence of ideas, these conflicts, fascinated me. I was also interested, though, in some of the critiques of mainstream notions of mental illness—Foucault, R.D. Laing, Thomas Szasz. These definitions can certainly be seen as contextual and contingent, culture-bound. Prinzhorn's book at least partly inspired Dubuffet's notion of *art brut*. My brother's illness, through my reading, crashed into *art brut*. I read Dubuffet for the first time, probably back in late '90s, and he was a terrific, passionate, and stylish critic of culture and art and elitism. Some of the writing is dated but I actually think if Dubuffet were alive and writing now he'd be quite critical of certain aspects of the outsider art world.

You've had some criticism from, and ensuing dialogue with, the artists whose work and lives you discuss in your book. Would you like to comment about that? Did you expect it?

I did expect that it was possible. People do not like to have their narratives taken over. I am very conscious of that and I tried to be as careful and as fair as possible while telling the story as I saw it, and I make the tricky ethics and pitfalls of documentary a central strain of inquiry in the book. On one level *The Colorful Apocalypse* is meta-nonfiction, a non-fiction partly about the difficulty of making "non-fiction". As Jonathan Raban has said, documentary can be "pastoral"—romanticized, sentimental depictions of the disenfranchised. And it is always class-bound: a maker from the socio-economic privileged class, a professor, say, visiting the fringes to report his findings back to the privileged class. Let's talk about those people. What do the lives of those people tell us. I of course come from where those people come from in this case; my grandparents were not so different from Howard Finster, William Thompson, or Myrtice West, if you took away some religiosity.

I liked and identified in many ways with the people I wrote about. The artists had very rigid senses of who they were; the outsider art world offered a different story of them; I saw them differently than they saw themselves and as the art world seemed to portray them. So there was, from the start, a mash-up of meanings. I assumed that as long I got the religious stuff these artists believed right, which was all they really seemed to care about while I was hanging out with them and interviewing them, they'd be fine with the book. And most people in the book are fine with it. I don't set out to kick people around. I enjoyed my time with these artists and did not mean my book as an attack on their beliefs or their art, and clearly most readers don't see it this way. I feel part of what my book suggests is that we all "shuffle our facts" to form a "straight line toward meaning"—i.e., we all construct our beliefs about who we are and what our lives mean in relation to our culture and society and express this in various ways. Outsider artists offer a pure and traceable expression of this process because of their single-minded devotion and belief and output of art, which constantly reissues a belief system in pictorial design (and sometimes eschatological writing, as was the case with the artists I visited). In my mind I was after ideas such as that rather than just human-interest journalism. Often when I read journalism, even really excellent journalism, I can't help but think about editorial slants, demographics, advertising, all the forces on the writing and the writer. Really I see the journalism of my book as part of a larger project that is an essay, an inquiry, an investigation into the making of meaning through creativity (perhaps delusion) in the face of dislocation and despair. All of the artists in the book have, to some extent, overcome difficult situations through their devotion to their calling and their art. What I didn't expect before the book came out was how my writing about a couple of the artists' visionary experiences and religious missions as an aspect of their psychology, a psychology very much in keeping with the narrative template, if you will, of many other "true" outsider artists and also in keeping with contemporary notions of psychosis (and Prinzhorn's earliest ideas), would so upset them. This is simply an obvious fact, and this assumption is common in most writing about outsider art and them. I make it clear that I'm an outsider to this art world, and that my views are simply my views, but I don't think you need to be a cultural theorist to get the sense that these artists are in complicated and institutionalized ways "exploited" within the outsider art world—in magazines like *Raw Vision* and in places like the American Visionary Art Museum—since they, the artists, assume curators and audiences are coming to hear and see their preaching, so to speak, when that is absolutely dismissed and perhaps patronized for a new message in the new art-world context of eccentric, anti-mainstream freedom. At times, at its worst, it struck me as almost tourism around the ill, disenfranchised, and marginalized. I don't mean to suggest that religious outsider artists aren't taken seriously within the outsider art world. I mean to say what I think is obvious—that they are not taken seriously in the way they think they are or would like to be taken seriously. At the time, I felt for them.

How do you balance the notion of making a book intriguing, perhaps contentious, and preserving the integrity of those you write about? Is that an issue?

It is an issue. But I guess intriguing, contentious, and fair are all in the eye of the beholder. I didn't intend contentious. I see it as bringing up a few thorny issues which might sting a few people. To me, though, that was simply about having the courage to report what seemed to me to be the truth of my travels and encounters. I tried always to be respectful to the artists, both personally and in the writing, but I had to balance that in the writing with saying what I felt had to be said to tell the story as I saw it.

I felt you'd been quite restrained in offering opinion or criticism about the artists and their work. Personally, I felt they all dug holes of varying depths and widths for themselves: there is no theological, artistic or philosophical construct behind what they are doing, it's all passion and polemic! Is there a place for those things in the world? At what point—if ever—is there justification for interfering or censoring?

I do actually think that each of the artists has a theological and philosophical construct behind what they do. But it is articulated through an "outsider" system of thinking and communication. Its modes are not always fully rational or easily followed if seen through a mainstream cultural lens, if we can define such a thing. Of course to these artists my construct, my thinking, is an "outsider" system. Outsider art institutions—magazines, journals, catalogues, galleries—regularly "interfere" with and "censor" some aspects of Christian fundamentalist outsider artists' core messages, which are sometimes about as politically incorrect as a message can be in our current cultural moment. One day I looked at work by a schizophrenic who makes incredibly disturbing, violent, pornographic collages, work by William Burroughs that had to do with morphine and addiction, and work by some Southern Christian "naïve" artists. In the secular art world the pornography and the drugs are fine (and never mind that Burroughs was way outside Roger Cardinal's or Dubuffet's definitions of this type of art), but the Christian messages had to be tempered and contextualized and shaped in the catalogue copy. They could only be presented if it was implicitly understood that the gallery did not necessarily agree with them, when this was not necessary around narcotics or pornographic, violent fantasy. I didn't want to offer easy judgment or opinion about these things so much as to report them as someone trying to be a thoughtful reader of culture. Personally I don't think any of these messages should be censored or softened.

Is your interest in the religious aspect of this kind of art simply because that is what is around you in the South USA, or is it what interests you? Your book of short prose, Sentimental, Heartbroken Rednecks, *seems to suggest that religion is still in the air, implicitly linking back to writers such as Flannery O'Connor.*

Religion is something, directly or indirectly, I write about often. Partly because I write about the place I come from. Partly because I grew up around religious obsession. Partly because I am interesting in storytelling, and I'm interested in how meaning—culturally and personally—is constructed (by a country, a sect, a region, a neighbourhood, a schizophrenic, an artist, a child, etc.). Back in grad school I was intrigued by some of the thinking of the Birmingham School of cultural studies—particularly Richard Hoggart and Stuart Hall. And lately I've been very interested in some personal writing by cultural anthropologists such as Michael Taussig, Alphonso Lingus, and Stephen Muecke, who write about myth and belief. I write quite autobiographically—perhaps annoyingly autobiographically—but autobiography for its own sake is of no interest to me. I like personal writing driven by intellectual inquiry, the self subordinate to the idea, open to its own confusion, the world's complexity, the way every story has counter-stories, how everyone involved in the story has a different version of it. You could say that every book I have written, almost every story and memoir and essay I have written, is essentially this: who is this person and how did this particularly person from this particular place and culture (or subculture) come to be who they are and do what they do or did?

My limited experience of the Southern States, including a visit to Howard Finster's sculpture garden, suggests that there is something strange at work. I mean it simply isn't normal when you meet people like Finster who has brothers and sisters falling down wells and being struck by lightning. Is it simply that society is stuck in a time-warp (I mean, Victorian England had a much higher mortality rate, lower life expectancy and larger families), or something else?

Partly it is religion, I think. Fundamentalist religion of any stripe tends to be anti-intellectual and anti-progress. And class—not just economics, but everything that goes with that, including especially literacy—is the great governing structure of America, but people outside of academia and progressive politics don't seem to go near that one. American mythology is powerful, and without a high-level of literacy one can't even begin to see the nature of the systems, institutions, myths, or sensibilities of one's own time and culture or think about how these things have come to be, how they shape who we are. Lewis Lapham published an essay many years ago about public education that pointed out that the perfect citizen for the American system of consumer capitalism was one educated enough to want and want and want and solvent enough to acquire and acquire and acquire (and if you don't have money, no worries—we have great credit cards with rates of 20% or so), but not educated enough to ask serious questions about the way we live. His kind of radical point, and a point others have made, was that a truly excellent public education system would go against consumer capitalism. Also religion, ritual, and tradition are particularly strong in the South, but I know many intellectuals and artists in the South (some devout Christians; in a complicated, existential way I myself am a Christian). There are wonderful universities and cities in the South. Some days I greatly miss Virginia and North Carolina, where I spent the first thirty years of my life. It's a complicated place like anywhere else. I recently read something suggesting that America is a continent pretending to be a country. The more I travel around the more I believe that. New England, the South, and the Southwest, for instance, may have less in common than England, Ireland, and Scotland.

The blurb on Sentimental, Heartbroken Rednecks *suggests the book "provocatively [blurs] the lines between autobiography, short fiction and essay." Is this correct? Might we be in the realms of creative-nonfiction here?*

Not sure if it is "provocative." It's an autobiographical book that moves from memoir to essay to little essayistic meta-fictions. Literary auto-biography is best understood as a contingent form, I think, housed in other forms—poems, essays, stories, biographies, journalism, memoir.

Is there a clear line between invention and reportage, between observation and critique? Does it matter? Is everything "fair game" for an author, or is there a moral duty to disguise, change or hide your sources in fiction? (I haven't read it, but I note that your first book, Angelhead, *is about your brother.)*

The lines are blurry in some cases—memoir in particular. My friend, a great writer, says memoir should be seen as autobiographical poetry is seen, since memory is a kind of "fiction", a "dream machine" that reshapes itself over time and as our identities and conceptions of self change as we age and go through life's events; not to mention all the living within cultural myths, technology, popular culture, etc. If telling your own story is easy, he would suggest, you can bet it is padded with delusion and that it resembles the truth only to you. If you think of great memoirs—Michael Ondaatje's *Running in the Family*, Maxine Hong Kingston's *The Woman Warrior*, John Edgar Wideman's *Brothers and Keepers*, English books like Blake Morrison's *When Did You Last See Your Father?* or Lorna Sage's *Bad Blood* or the autobiographical vignettes in Alan Bennett's *Untold Stories*—it is clear that those texts are mixes of memory and imagination, recounting and creation, observation and speculation. That's what memoir is. The past cannot be fully recovered. It requires some form of invention. Once memory and encounter are made into narrative they start to become "fictionalized", even while your mission is to pursue with rigour and intelligence the "truth" of a situation, and you don't need to be Derrida to understand that. But I'm interested in reporting, in an imaginative and subjective way, about the world I live in. I think one has a real obligation to the facts especially when writing about other, real people. In those cases, such as in *The Colorful Apocalypse*, I travel, talk to people, use tapes, transcripts, notes, do research, keep a big folder of articles and photographs, try to know the background of my subject(s), try make sure the manuscript is carefully checked. As I have seen, though, even with all that your work will be absolute fiction to someone. I can pretty much assure you that if the farmers in Agee's *Let Us Now Praise Famous Men* or the miners in Orwell's *The Road to Wigan Pier* ever read those books, they said something along the lines of "what is this crap? I like me job!"

Is this mix of genres "provocative" as the blurb suggests, or is that marketing talk from the publishers?

You're making me regret that word! Assuming the world is this complex place I seem to think it is, then maybe the old conventions of genre can't hold what needs to be said as well as they used to. I think of writers like Lydia Davis, Geoff Dyer, W.G. Sebald, some of the prose of Czesław Miłosz or Charles Simic. The French writer Jean-Paul Kauffman's or Cees Nooteboom's travelogues. What are those wonderful things they make—poems, stories, novels, essays, profiles, travelogues, philosophy, journalism, parable, fable? Also, it is worth us at this late date thinking about for instance what freedom a novelist or poet has, what constraints but also authority a journalist has, how memoir is certainly widely popular to some extent because at this time we are interested in confessional and testimony and cleansing rituals. (I think of the great scene in J.M. Coetzee's *Disgrace* where he must confess his sins to the authorities to save his academic post; maybe no scene in a novel signifies the contemporary moment as well as that one in my mind.)

It is suggested that the fifteen prose pieces of Sentimental, Heartbroken Redneck *accumulate and interact to provide a "meditation on the nature of, and necessity for, storytelling itself." Certainly, something I teach my first year students—before we get to fragmentation, hypertext and postmodernism!—is that we make sense of the world through narratives, and that we can only filter, edit and select from what we experience ourselves. This works both ways: it both denies authorial invention, but also says everything can be utilised as source &/or subject. Where do you stand on that?*

I guess it depends on the project. In my first book, a memoir, I stayed tight to the facts and did research but "invented" a depiction of my brother's mind in psychotic state based on what I knew from living with him. I also, though, call attention to this speculation/'invention' on my part, let the reader see what I'm doing and hopefully understand why and even how I'm doing it. I also hold up the "truth" as I see it against newspaper accounts, which were "untrue" in some ways while having gotten all the facts they used correct. In the last section of *Sentimental, Heartbroken Redneck*, the fictional pieces all use facts and actual events as starting points but then veer toward pure invention, keep pointing out how facts fail us or tell only a little of what we need. I would only call that fiction, but you can see how close to the line I am when I'm on either side of it. *The Colorful Apocalypse* was an attempt, if we divorce form from content for a moment, to pull apart the mechanics of searching out story, fact, and incident. The book is actually structured as the story of a writer traveling around collecting information to write a book—a fraught endeavour, one that might actually be upsetting to some whose interests are at odds with the writer's interest. But each episode and scene depicts the actual interaction, the actual conversation—I knew the people in the book would read the book and judge it—thus the tapes and transcripts, the notes and photos I took so that I could accurately describe clothing, rooms, what people said and did, their accents, how they moved, etc. But of course it is consciously a literary construction, a creation. I use and narrate only what I need to make the book, to tell the "truth" of the situations, characters, and interactions as I experienced them. But given these factors you can see—I can see—how people who don't give a hoot about literature, or don't know anything about literature, don't live in it the way I do, don't think about the "nature of narrative", who are more interested in or connected to the topic of outsider art, would say, "Hey, this isn't an academic book, or a coffee-table book, or cultural history, or straight newspaper/magazine profiles. Who does jackass Greg Bottoms think he is?"

Greg Bottoms, *The Colorful Apocalypse. Journeys in Outsider Art*, (Chicago: University of Chicago Press, 2007)
Greg Bottoms, *Sentimental, Heartbroken Rednecks. Stories from the New South* (Washington, DC: Shoemaker Hoard, 2nd edition, 2007)

[*WiTH* 4 and *Stride*, 2007]

John Burnside's *Gift Songs*

John Burnside is a prolific and talented author. This new volume of poetry comes hot on the heels of last year's superb *Selected Poems* and is published alongside *The Devil's Footprints*, a fifth novel. The "gift song" is a concept taken from Shaker aesthetic, and the book's content is flagged up in the blurb as "faith and connection, the community of living creatures and the idea of a free church—where faith is placed, not in dogma or a possible credo, but in the indefinable".

Burnside's early poems were often about the edges of civilization: the suburbs and other hidden or forgotten places, and the characters and narrators who inhabit these regions. Slowly, notions of epiphany, faith/ doubt, and a sense of community and wonder have entered the poems, often in an elliptical and hinted-at manner. Now, however, it seems Burnside is unafraid to name the absences, the unknown, in terms of the spiritual; indeed, *Gift Songs* is full of theological argument and debate.

The book starts with four 'Responses to Augustine of Hippo', long poems recalling "the shift in a long conversation" and "the seep of music through the bone; / a wavelength of owls where everything is static". Its is unclear whether this is

>   lifeblood
>   or rapture
>   taken for a song

but as Burnside discusses and describes "The shapes we mistake / for love", we are drawn into a world of small wonders and remembered moments, into a creation that reflects the hands and mind of its unknown creator. The narrator has "a sense of someone waking in the dark", someone "puzzled / by something he ought to remember." Resurrection, time, life itself, bewilder the narrator here, whose life is only made liveable only by a series of epiphanies and the music of language itself as he conjures up evidence for and against St Augustine's theology. This is beautiful writing, full of sharp and precise images, dynamic and intriguing thought.

The final 'Four Quartets' obviously contain a nod to T.S. Eliot, and they too are a response to string quartets (this time by Bartók and Britten). They are also an exploration of place and home, both literally and as a metaphor for faith. In a way these poems, each subdivided into several numbered sections, continue the trajectory of the Augustine poems, but for me they have lost a lot of the music of the first poems and instead drift toward abstract debate: what they say is interesting, how they say it often isn't. Thankfully, the fourth poems sees Burnside back on form, declaring his belief that

> whether we pray
> to a god, or the weight of an absence,
> what matters it the way the story runs
>
> forever,
> through the fields of transformation

This transformation accounts for the narrator's awareness of "the god of silt and shipwreck smeared across / the clouded glass" and elsewhere, and an engagement and acceptance of

>   joy—
> which is neither happiness, nor triumph
> and cannot come from anything
> but passing through the white of dissolution;

This joy leads the speaker home—

> but home is where everything happens: panic and joy,
> the meeting with the god, that stink of goat;
> hairless angels stepping from the rain;

and toward a closing vision of [re?]creation,

> where bodies formed, great waves of sound and light
> becoming fingers, eyelids, shoulders, hair.

In between these sequences of poems, is a section of three groups of poems. The middle group, 'Five Animal Poems', are slight and out of place, but 'Varieties of Religious Experience' and 'For a Free Church' both feed into and from the work I've already discussed. 'Varieties' are shorter lyric poems with specific titles such as 'Liturgy', 'Conversion' and 'Afterlife'. 'Prayer' finds the narrator

hoarse with the promise of song
and the grace notes of terror

while by the eleventh, final poem 'Lares' he is "bright in the here and now, and unencumbered."

'For a Free Church' is briefer and it's content less clear, concerned with "the quiet that runs in the grass" and "gold in the seams of my hand". Here faith is vague, is only "the lull of gospel" hanging around "home and kirk".

Burnside may not name his faith *per se* in these poems, but his evocation and exploration of the world around us, and his willingness to ask questions of the unknown creator, of himself and of the reader, make for genuine, intelligent poetry that takes literary and philosophical risks. *Gift Songs* is very much a precious gift, one that we as readers should not refuse.

[*Third Way*, May 2007]

John Burnside

Aggressive Interview #1: Rupert Loydell

Gists & Piths: The "avant garde", "experimentalism" in poetry, all that stuff: waste of time, yes?

Rupert Loydell: Not at all. My own inclination would be that the avant-garde is where interesting stuff happens and then in due course filters back into the mainstream. Media and literature are fickle things and what is derided at the time often turns up later to surprise us: see, for instance cut-ups and collage and the '90s phenomenon of mash-ups in music.

But the people who care about experiments in language, they don't matter, do they, in a wider society?

Who is to say what affects society? I don't know anyone who is out to "change the world", more that they are interested in language. On a personal level I've learnt that being able to be approachable and talk about my work in plain English wins over audiences.

So who actually matters when it comes to reading poetry? Why?

Anyone who is pushing boundaries. We all need amusing and entertaining, but the things that change the world are films/music/poems/novels that challenge us and make people think. On the poetry front, I for one am tired of shaggy-dog poems with a punch line. I'm far more intrigued by the big projects of Rachel Blau DuPlessis, Tony Lopez and Charles Olson.

There is an implication in some circles that without experimentation coming from the margins into wider society, society would stagnate. (Well, it's an idea I put forward in classes for debate.) But a common criticism of the avant garde is that it has sometimes (e.g. Eliot, Pound, et al, pre-World War 2, or Mottram, Griffiths, et al, 1970s) taken disproportionate control of mainstream channels in order to promote minority interests, to the detriment of wider readerships. You say, "Who is to say what affects society?" but this is an example of someone taking the reigns and controlling. This is bad, yes?

If people understand how language (or paint, or photography, whatever) works then they can understand a wide variety of art forms. Postmodernism suggests linear narratives & histories are an outdated construct and that lots happens simultaneously and in a network. I would agree with this notion.

I would also argue that we live in an age of more and more diversity and smaller and smaller audiences. We can do what we want and probably find an audience for it. I don't know many poets, avant-garde or not, chasing fame and fortune. They, and I count myself in this, simply want their work read—and, in the main, the internet now facilitates that process.

Society and the media manipulate and are manipulated. That seems the way of things to me. I'm inclined towards democratic anarchy and individual responsibility—the latter means I would encourage people to think for themselves and engage with life in the fullest sense, including the arts.

I don't really want to get into a Mottram and Griffiths debate again. I think the Poetry Society saga they were involved in has been blown out of all proportion by both sides. I am on record elsewhere, and am happy to be so again, saying that actually in the late 70s and early 80s the exciting poetry stuff was happening elsewhere in London anyway. I didn't expect the Poetry Society to be relevant or exciting, there was too much improvised music & film, performance poetry, postpunk music, and exciting visual arts and dance/performance theatre going on to worry about damp rooms in Earls Court, or who was controlling the duplicator in the basement.

You say "the avant garde is where the interesting stuff happens", but this is relative. If the "interesting stuff" is only interesting to a minority, then surely it is merely "stuff that interests geeks"? You point out that some stuff does cross over, like cut up and collage techniques, which implies that the geeks get left behind. Do you think geeks deserve more recognition for what they do, or should they continue to work in obscurity and let people with a better understanding of the mainstream carry their ideas across to society? And why?

Who you calling a geek? As I said in my last answer, the world has more and more small networks. I'm happy in my network[s] of readers, colleagues, friends, publishers, students and fellow writers. Human beings all have different tastes, and that's fine.

We all need entertaining at times—so sometimes I watch TV and sometimes I like funny rhyming poetry—but I can't abide people telling me they are writers when they don't understand how language works and what it can do. You don't have to like Jackson Mac Low or Charles Bernstein's poetry, but it's not incomprehensible: if you move beyond content, the poems work in the same ways that mainstream poets do. That is the work is constructed with language, with words, deliberately organised and arranged for the viewer (even if a chance procedure has been used in the writing process).

I always get my students to approach a poem with that in mind, to accept it as finished work the way the author wanted it—and to engage with how it has been made and what it might be doing, then on to content and what it says, and lastly whether or not they like it (which I'm not that interested in anyway; we're usually looking at poems to find out about poems, not the students' tastes).

And to close, a two part question about "shaggy dog poems with a punch line": Why are you tired of them? And, given the prevalence of this kind of work in current publishing, doesn't this suggest that it has more importance to poetry's readership than you give credit for? [I'm thinking partly of Pound's loathing of "How to write" manuals, but his feeling that there was something a student of language and writing could learn from them—but what?]

I'm confused that you think marketing and mainstream publishing has anything to do with readership? We all know the "big" publishers don't sell a lot of poetry books apart from a few authors (Carol Ann Duffy, Roger McGough, Ted Hughes, etc). It's fashion and marketing, and I don't worry about it.

I've played some of those games in the past as a publisher, sometimes to good effect, but basically they absorb a lot of time and effort that can be better used actually publishing work and getting readers. More than ever, with print-on-demand and the internet, and the current state of the mainstream book trade, it's easier than ever to sell books and find readers. However, it's harder than ever to break the financial and fashionable strangleholds of the publishers who cling to the outdated publishing model of warehousing long print-runs, and investing huge amounts of money supporting teams of staff and wining & dining competition judges. Those days are gone. Salt and Shearsman prove it—they are currently where the poetry powerhouses are.

As for why I don't like poems that are shaggy dog stories... I don't want to know answers, I want more questions. I don't want to empathise with an author, I want to be told something new. I don't want confession, polemic, opinions, wise thoughts or epiphanies. I think there are more interesting things to be said and more interesting ways to say them. That probably makes me a geek in your reference terms above, but I can honestly say I want poems to challenge, excite, confuse and astound me. Small-minded narrative squibs usually don't do any of that. I like poems I can return to time and time again; that continue to befuddle and confound, amuse and irritate me.

I really do think that works, such as *The Waste Land* and *The Cantos*, Berryman's *Dream Songs*, *The Maximus Poems* and others, last because they can't be pinned down, however many books get written about them. They continue to intrigue, because of their very ambition, complexity and language. We need more ambitious writers—whether they are revitalising a traditional form (there seems to be a spate of sonneteers around at the moment) or creating their own projects. Rachel Blau DuPlessis's *Drafts* project is just such an intriguing and ambitious work; Robert Sheppard's *Twentieth Century Blues* project also.

[*Gists & Piths*, 2008]

Accessible & Accountable

An Interview with Rupert Loydell

GEOMETER: *You said in an interview recently that although your writing is experimental, you have found that in talking about your work, finding a simple language and mode of address is the best way to reach people. A lot of the poems in your latest collection are experimental, whilst retaining a simplicity of language. Have you found that a tension in your own work, between pushing language and experimenting with it, and that need to remain accessible and accountable?*

RUPERT LOYDELL: I think there is a tension there, but my working practice is rooted in collage and procedural devices… my vocabulary is deliberately everyday; and I tend to smooth my syntax down. I'm not that interested in revealing the way I make my work, it's just a tool like any other.

A lot of the poems in An Experiment in Navigation *are quite reflexive, frequently making reference to the poem itself, and the circumstances of its composition, or even its potential reception. Often these techniques seem to be a way of drawing the reader's attention to the limits of the poem, or its shortcomings. To what extent do you write out of this sense of anxiety?*

I want people to be aware of how the world is constructed by the language we use to describe and record our experiences. I quite like jogging the reader to think about what they are actually experiencing: words, in a specific order, in a specific layout, on a printed page. I don't think I've ever thought about it highlighting a poem's shortcomings (not that I'm claiming all my work is brilliant, you understand)—I think that's an interesting idea.

I suppose I was thinking of "the poem" in general, as in all poems, in the sense of the poem (and by extension I suppose language) as a form. I wanted to ask whether you struggled with the notion that perhaps the poem as a vehicle is sometimes inadequate to record experience.

I don't think I'm primarily interested in poems as records of experience… that sounds a little too like narrative and epiphany for me. I'm more interested in them as a language construct, sometimes a quite abstract one, at other times more linear or experiential.

Since I believe we only think in words—that is everything we experience we turn into language—then no, I feel poems can be up to the job. But I think we are likely to need complexity and depth in the poems to deal with experience at any level beyond the immediate or simple.

A lot of the poems come back to the notion of religious faith and belief. There is a great line in which you describe faith as "a rain-flushed stream overflowing into doubt". Is this something you are trying to work through in the poems, the navigation of that porous border between faith and doubt?

O yes, it's a recurring and ongoing theme. How to deal with the Christian faith in a secular and post-religious age. How to believe when belief for so many people seems to be synonymous with war, capitalism, polemic and oppression. The poet and songwriter Sydney Carter says it best for me:

DOUBT IS

Doubt is what you
drown in or walk upon
the solid deck
is never really solid

singing a carol round
the Christmas tree
you can forget that you
are floating but

the ship is not rock-bottomed
all the while
you walk upon the water
I will love

this dark and
downward pulling
angel doubt
that I could never learn

to dance without.

I'm no dancer, but I understand that underlying tension in life

In 'The Poem I Do Not Want To Read' you describe that very poem: a poem seemingly engaged with a world that most of us are fortunately quite effectively insulated from. A world of loss, and of "wars", and the "madness" that these other worlds breed. The resultant poem you describe as being "more than language". Is this another form of anxiety? An anxiety over how poetry, and language can describe a world that is seemingly beyond and bigger than language?

Yes, but that poem is very much a response to the way David Grubb voiced those concerns in his own poetry recently. I found myself ridiculously moved by what in many ways is the kind of poetry I dislike: narrative, epiphanic and with a "message" to convey. David has worked as an aid worker and is interested in conveying those experiences—he's been in a couple of times to university to talk to our students about transforming and re-presenting personal experience. I found myself bemused by my emotional response and moved to write a kind of riposte.

A lot of poets are interested in, or at least troubled by aspects of politics, foreign affairs, the state of the world. You touched on it yourself in the question about faith (it being conflated with "war, capitalism and oppression".) And yet not many poets write about this, or if they do, they engage at the level of content, and not at a stylistic level. So what can happen is that you get polemic, or sloganeering (I do not include David in this). Do you think David's poem will perhaps jolt you to consider writing other sorts of poems?

I'm very much against polemical poems, simply because if/when polemic is needed I tend to think there are better ways to get a message across to a wider audience (posters, tv, films, photography etc). I think that I've always written about politics, theology, belief and politics, but implicitly rather than explicitly (ignoring my juvenilia, that is!).

I know David quite well and am a fan of his work. I'm envious of his ability to skirt polemic and write issues based poetry in the way he does. But of course he draws on the experimental side of poets like W.S. Graham and East European writers, and isn't just shouting at or explaining his concerns to his readers.

I think 'The Poem I do Not Want to Read' is about as near as I will get to polemic for a while. There's also a poem about the Holocaust and my experience of the Imperial War Museum exhibition in one of my bluechrome books.

You teach poetry as well as write it. We ran an interview with James Byrne (editor of The Wolf *poetry magazine) in which he suggested that new young poets are not sufficiently daring, and tend to imitate their forebears, rather than taking risks on writing something new and original. What's your view on what is animating students in their writing, both in terms of the content and the styles they employ?*

I think in many ways I would agree with James Byrne, but I do think that you have to let people deal with form and poetics in their own way. My students are actually far more immersed in media theory and cultural theory than I ever was at that age, and they resist many of the ideas we discuss. For instance, in response to Robert Sheppard's notion in 'The Education of Desire' that language has been debased by advertising and that therefore revolutionary poetry needs to use language in a different way, my students tend to 1) disagree that language has been debased and 2) see no need to write revolutionary poetry anyway, let alone fracture syntax! Many of my students are interested in reinvigorating more conventional forms, seeing if they can't go back and make ideas such as sonnets work again. They're not alone, obviously, if we look at the work in the recent Reality Street anthology of sonnets. I'm happy to think that maybe we've gone beyond the fallout of the 1960s revolution and divide in British poetry and can now take on board, and use many ideas. I see that happening a lot in the USA where it seems Language poetries are reinvigorating the lyric; that's now starting to happen over here, too. There's no reason that other generations, groups or individuals are going to engage with the same work that I do. What we can do is be open and encourage them to read widely. I do think the new century has seen a lot of re-assessment and republication of many types of work by many different authors, so that anybody who is paying attention can now see a very different 20th century poetry than one could say in the mid '80s. I also think we can see that many lecturers and teachers in universities and schools now who re critically engaged with more experimental writing; obviously, this will have an effect on pupils and students as they come through various English and Creative Writing courses.

I remember reading an interview you did with Iain Sinclair in which you asked him whether he thought poetry had ever been, or ever could be popular. I know you have talked in the past about the fragmentation of audiences, and the positive aspect of this—poets finding their own audiences. But do you think there is a limit to this? To be blunt, does it matter if nobody is reading?

I think that people *are* reading, but they probably aren't buying books. I know from my experiences with *Stride* that online poetry magazines have many, many more readers than the paper edition ever had; and even more so than the sales of our poetry books when we were publishing those. Because I paint, I'm used to a canvas being exhibited once or twice then sold—it disappears out of my life, leaving only a photo or catalogue image. Poems aren't like that, I can file the original and send many electronic or paper copies of it out into the world. I remain absurdly optimistic about online readership and networks of critics and friends—after ten years I know my poems are read by more people than ever. Meanwhile, the few hundred sales of my books stay pretty consistent. I obviously can't imagine writing if nobody ever read it, but then again I know several authors who do pretty much write for themselves and themselves alone. So who knows?

What are your student's expectations about who will be reading their work, and where they might publish it?

I don't teach on a vocational course, it's more about creative writing being a useful tool for English students, so I can't really answer that. Some publish online and we have a magazine for our English with degrees that I put together two or three times a year. I'm certainly careful not to raise any false expectations, nor let them naïvely think that having a Faber or Bloodaxe book means sales, readers, fame, employability or critical reception.

I think we are entering an era where many art forms are financially worthless. They have a cultural value, but we may have to rethink how we use them, or even think about them. It's happened in poetry, and you can see it happening to the music biz: you can download any music from the last 50 or 60 years for nothing and listen to it. The record companies could have chosen to distribute their archives in small CD runs (or even CDR form), for small amounts of money, instead they have kept up the pretext that you need to sell millions of copies of anything to make it viable. They've been proved wrong, and they have missed out.

Much as I like books, I still understand a lot of reading goes on online, and a lot of critical debate and dialogue happens by email. The world has changed, poetry dissemination has or must too.

As you mention, you are a practicing painter as well as a poet. I'd be interested to hear how the concerns you have as a writer relate to those you have as a painter? In other words, is there a cross-over in terms of what animates you, and keeps you curious in both, or are they quite separate in your mind?

I think they remain fairly separate these days, although I can see analogous processes such as layering, collage and quotation, as well as the fact I work in series, in common. Even though I talk about the substance of language to my students, and try to persuade them what a fantastic medium it is to play and experiment with, I know that the physical substance of oil paint is very different to words on the page, as is colour. I probably draw more on contemporary improvised and classical music for ideas for shape and form more than painting, and singer-songwriters for ideas of the lyrical. Having said that I have recently completed a fourth 'Ballads of the Alone' sequence, 'Different Chemistry', which engage with photography—in this case the work of Joel-Peter Witkin. (The first three 'Ballads' were in my book *A Conference of Voices*.)

What are you reading at the moment?

Craig Dworkin's anthology *The Consequence of Innovation: 21st Century Poetics*; a new book on Ad Reinhardt by Michael Corris; the Tate catalogue on Francis Bacon; poetry collections by H.L. Hix,Paige Ackerson-Kiely, John Taggart, Juliana Spahr, Mark Jarman, Geoffrey O'Brien, Michael Brennan, John Wilkinson, Bruce Beasley and Alex Lemon; Reginald Shepherd's *Lyric Postmodernisms: an Anthology of Contemporary Innovative Poetries*; the QAA assessment criteria, as our degrees at Falmouth are under review; and the first ten of Olson's *Maximus Poems* as I am supervising a dissertation on it.

[*Geometer*, 2008]

Writing the Unknown

The Poetry of David Miller

David Miller is a poet who is concerned with the process of writing, although he seems to have drawn on different writers to such contemporaries as Ken Edwards and Robert Sheppard for inspiration. (In a 1983 interview [Crouch, 1994, p6] he mentions that he "started writing when I was fourteen or fifteen [having] discovered certain authors who excited me—writers as various as Arp and Dante and Henry Miller", and later [p6] says "In the years immediately after my first attempts as a writer, Nerval and Malcolm Lowry were probably most influential.") He also seems to want to use *process* with more regard to the "content" of his work.

Later [p9] in the same interview he is asked if he "could… say something about montage?" He replies:

> Montage—at least as I employ it myself—has to do with setting up relationships and connections—or with destroying familiar, conventional connections—in a direct way, by putting one thing next to another (or—to think of it in the sense of *movement*—one thing after another). The materials involved can be very disparate, or they can be more continuous in relation to one another, the juxtapositions more subtle

and goes on to stress that

> the main thing is that something is disclosed—some depth or "surplus" of meaning, or some angle of vision—which was not available before, at least in quite the same way.

Whilst the relationships and connections Miller sets up may be complex and unfamiliar, and the reader may—as Sheppard has suggested—be asked to work harder and make the poem, Miller stresses, in a later interview with Andrew Bick [Bick, 1994, p35] that

> whenever you put one thing against another you're establishing a connection, even if the two things are discontinuous

and also [p35] that he is

> both establishing connections between things and bringing
> meaning out of those connections, and also bringing things
> together in such a way that familiar connections are displaced

In 'The Poetics of David Miller', an essay in the same book, Robert Sheppard
[1994a, p17] describes this way of working as 'Broken Sequences':

> Not the regularity of building bricks, blocks structuring a façade,
> a barrier. Nor the almost seamless studio edits of Miles Davis ...
> splicing like with like. But something like slow montage, fading
> and wiping, fading up again with a fresh image.

Sheppard [p 16] also quotes an earlier description by Ken Edwards [1988,
p269], where he describes Miller's ability "to make the discontinuities and
spaces in his work shine with the unsaid", suggesting that the the links
between these things are both spaces/gaps *and* connections.

This is shown well by a poem in Miller's book *Stromata* [Miller, 1995].
'Moments' [pp39-40] consists of three short sections, which I shall quote
in full:

> Graph of durations: grid on which we move. Cut
> each line on the grid down, down to where thought
> stops. *When a line is cut into many parts, no matter
> how many the parts, something will be left. One can
> never cut into the last unit.*

> •

> "The hare will never conclude the race which is
> his love—each moment is divided, cut down further,
> close to impossibility. He runs and is still." Ah yes;
> my hand reaches toward you, reaches and will not
> reach. Yet even in the photograph, how evident that
> water has already bathed the wound.

> •

Perhaps it's that very moment when the child
raises her head, with its shock of auburn hair, to
look up at the sky; a look that's immediately cancelled by the sun's too-intense brightness.

Or perhaps it's another selection of time, not an
afternoon's blue, but a dawn completely red, orange.

Cry out in the midst of it.

The first part of the poem sets up an abstraction, asks that we consider "duration", time, as a grid, a graph against which we can be seen to move. It also instructs us to take this concept of time and consider where it becomes the smallest possible fragment, the moment where "thought stops". He contrasts this with the geometrical concept of the irreducibility of line, here in italic, which states that the smallest possible line is still a line. The reader is left to come to the conclusion that perhaps the smallest moment of time, is still a moment of time.

The next section begins with a quotation (whose source is not given) which continues to consider the concept of small units of time, but makes them specific to a hare racing. It suggests that if time is considered in this way, even though the smallest moment always exists, that a race being run in this way will never end—the moments of time are too small, the racing hare "runs and is still".

"Ah yes" says the narrator, and drags us back into another time-zone where he "reaches toward" an unspecified "you". But again, in similar manner to the racing hare, the hand "reaches and will not reach", the moment under consideration is too small to allow the movement to occur.

Then there seems to be a jump in both subject and time. The narrator considers a photograph, presumably of the narrator reaching out his hand, and draws our attention to "how evident [it is] that water has already bathed the wound."

We are left to make sense of this time slippage and second-hand information, but the third section quickly draws us in with its "Perhaps it's that very moment...". We do not know whether it refers us back to the moment in the photograph we have just read, or the moment "when the child raises her head" it goes on to describe, or—most likely—both, which may or may not be concurrent. Either way the time theme continues with the moment of the child "look[ing] up at the sky" "immediately cancelled by the sun's too intense brightness". Is the photographic image over-exposed, does the girl turn from the bright light, or does the viewer of the event, be it the poem's narrator us the reader? We do not know, and it seems the poem's narrator does not want us to. The poems goes on to tell us "it's another selection of time, not an afternoon's blue"—as we might assume from the "sun's too-intense brightness"—but a dawn completely red, orange.'

Not only has the frozen moment slipped from happening in the present tense to become a photographic memory, the moment of writing—and therefore us reading—has been altered, too. By a trick of writing we are moved from sunlit afternoon to the morning sun rising; or maybe even that is too specific, for "perhaps it's another selection of time"? The poem's narrator is perhaps keen to have us consider the moments of time he has introduced to us as a concept as interchangeable, or available, that we might be able to "both establish connections between things and bring meaning out of those connections".

The strange thing is that in the final sentence of the poem we are instructed to "Cry out in the midst of it." Is this a cry in the dawn light, an echoed cry of pain from the wound in the poem's second part, or a cry of despair, or perhaps elation, at the discovery that time is fluid and elastic? All of these, I suggest. Miller has successfully laid out several ideas and images and allowed us to link and consider them in various ways, and led us toward an epiphanic moment of release: the cry we are instructed to make.

In a review in *The Many Review*, Paul Green [1983, p30] suggests that "Because the poetry of David Miller is so simple it must be approached with caution." Robert Hampson [1997, p ix] has also commented on "The simple language", noting that it, along with "the collaging of sentences and phrases, the interplay between sentences and phrasal units remain a characteristic of Miller's work."

What is interesting is that it is this simple language which Miller utilises within his montage process to try and enter, and presumably encourage the reader to enter, "into what, with regard to reason, can only be regarded as a darkness—where one doesn't *know*." [Bick, 1994, p36]. He equates this state of unknowing to a "negative theology", where one can only discover anything about God by what we don't know. In fact Miller says, again in his interview with Bick [1994, p36], that his "interest in that tradition, or at least as it relates to art and writing, is specifically to do with notions of unknowing, of a process in which one suspends any sort of rational certainty...". One can presume then that the tentative connections made as one reads 'Moments' [above] are deliberate, that Miller wants us to deduce for ourselves, to know by not knowing.

Indeed, it seems that Miller considers the poems themselves as tentative. In a cover blurb written for an early volume of his poems, *The Caryatids* [Miller, 1975, inside cover flap], he writes:

> These poems are a starting point: they try to remain open to the more complex compounds of vision, emotion and thought... many concepts and devices have been evolved from an interest in modern music, painting and cinema.

Interestingly enough, Tim Allen [1996], reviewing *Stromata*, suggests that "the more Miller does not tell us the more the reader seems to know", suggesting that this tentativeness serves its purpose. Norman Jope [1992] agrees, asserting that Miller's work "is a delicate, allusive web of perceptual textures, interspersed with flashing personal epiphanies..." with a "painterly awareness of the passages of colour, light and shadow."

I like the fact that Miller draws on personal memories, and ideas from painting and theology; I share many of his interests and concerns. I like his seriousness and purpose, too. I believe he is still "linguistically innovative" despite the fact he has declared [Bick, 1994, p37] that he doesn't "see what [he is] doing as a writer as enclosed by language in any reductionist sense."

Douglas Messerli [1984, p148] might, surprisingly, be seen to be in agreement, at the end of an interview:

> MESSERLI: ...Language is truth. Language makes meaning. Language is meaning. And that signifies that to write a poem is to shoulder immense responsibility. As a poet, can one afford to accept the world as it is? Mustn't one work with the reader to try to recomprehend it, to reshape it?

> INTERVIEWERS: Is there something to which language—or language artefacts—should be faithful, responsive? Language itself?

> MESSERLI: To language in action, which is life.

It might be argued that if "Language is meaning" there can be nothing unknown as Miller suggests, or that "language is only made possible by the immaterial" [Bick, 1994, p36]. Interestingly enough, Language poet Lyn Hejinian, an author in fact published by Messerli, discusses this idea of knowing through language [Hejinian, 1994], and—to my mind, importantly—seems more tentative than an initial reading might suggest (my italics for emphasis):

> Language discovers what one *might* know. Therefore, the limits of language are the limits of what we might know. [p653]

Indeed, she goes on [p654] to say

> Because we have language we find ourselves in a peculiar relationship to the objects, events, and situations which constitute what we imagine of the world. Language generates its own characteristics in the human psychological and spiritual condition.

Later [p654] she suggests that we are often overwhelmed by our:

> …experience of the vastness and uncertainty of the world and by what often seems to be the inadequacy of the imagination that longs to know it, and for the poet, the even greater inadequacy of the language that appears to describe, discuss or disclose it

Yet, it seems to me, Miller bypasses that with his ability to explore what is unknowable by writing about the known. I'm sure he is aware of the fact that, as Hejinian [1994, p654] puts it:

> The progress of a line or sentence, or a series of lines or sentences, has spatial properties as well as temporal properties.

and also that

> Language itself is never in a state of rest. … I mean both intellectually and emotionally active.

Miller has certainly put the concepts of spatial and temporal properties (or what we might in this instance call memory) to good use in his writing, as in this excerpt from an untitled poem [the twelfth, the book is unpaginated] in *Appearance & Event* [Miller, 1977]:

> If the images of friends have returned,
> returned, in public places, where & when
> they were not,   could I call this
> a superimposition   of two systems, two
> material planes?   Is it confusion,
> or some sort of clarity? —Certainly
> there was, in each case, light   attendant...
>
> This ghostliness may, in fact, be the very
> stuff of form– The *light waves travel*
> *through completely empty space.*   You
> make an appearance or   I appear:
> like a superimposition
> of single images,
> the shapes pile up   in a structure:
>
> but, instead, the movement is like a signal-beam
> travelling the length
> & the attraction grows.
>
> Wind—or the fiery mind.

Here, again, scientific phenomena are countered with memories, apparitions and mystical events to help the poet consider the idea of "two systems" or "two material planes" intersecting. Miller is interested in how we can bend, use and move beyond language. He suggests [1977, third poem] that

> Our strength is to transform
> the image
> a suddenness,
> is an endurance. We use a term
> like "water" even when
> there is none, &
> the language sustains
> the meaning of the term.

We build   situations,
where we watch ourselves

electricity through the images;
talking, we built a house &
we watched ourselves

talking…

Whether we watch ourselves via the medium of film or television, as
the "electricity through the images" might suggest, or through poetic
transformation, Miller [1977, eleventh poem] wishes to subvert both time
and language, existence itself:

…Even
our materiality is an endurance: void
shot through with brilliant splinters of duration

Time, for Miller, is a series of epiphanies, "brilliant splinters" in the dark/
void; the tiniest moments of time and memory possible, stacked and built
up in different juxtaposition for the reader to assemble his own meaning,
help fuel their own "fiery mind[s]".

Works Cited

Allen, T., (1994) (review of *Stromata*) in *Terrible Work* 6, p47, Plymouth, Spineless.

Bick, A., (1994), 'An Interview with David Miller, 1992' in *At the Heart of Things: the poetry and prose of David Miller*, pp35-41, Exeter, Stride.

Crouch, J., (1994), 'An Interview with David Miller, 1983' in *At the Heart of Things: the poetry and prose of David Miller*, pp6-15, Exeter, Stride.

Edwards, K., (1988), 'Some Younger Poets: Introduction' in *The New British Poetry 1968-88*, pp16-19, London, Paladin.

Green, P., (1983), (Review of *Unity*) in *The Many Review* 1, pp30-31, London, The Many Press.

Hampson, R., (1997), 'Foreword' in David Miller's *Collected Poems*, pp viii-xxii, Salzburg, University of Salzburg Press.

Hejinian, L., (1994), 'from 'The Rejection of Closure' ' in *Postmodern American Poetry*, pp653-658, New York, Norton.

Jope, N., (1992), (Review of *Pictures of Mercy* and *The Break*) in *Memes* 7, Plymouth, Memes.

Messerli, D., (1984), 'Language in Action: An Interview with Douglas Messerli' in *Gargoyle* 24, pp136-148, Washington DC, Paycock Press.

Miller, D., (1975), *The Caryatids: Poems 1971-73*, London, Enitharmon Press.

Miller, D., (1977), *Appearance & Event: 16 poems: 1976*, Paraparauma, Hawk Press

Miller, D., (1995) *Stromata*, Providence, Burning Deck.

Miller, D., (1997), *Collected Poems*, Salzburg, University of Salzburg Press.

Sheppard, R., (1994a), 'A Gap at the Heart of Things: The Poetics of David Miller' in *At the Heart of Things: the poetry and prose of David Miller*, pp16-20, Exeter, Stride.

[*Golden Handcuffs Review*, Vol. 1, No. 10, 2008]

So Many Unsaids

An interview with Paul Sutton

Rupert Loydell: *Paul, why are your poems so angry?*

Paul Sutton: I guess I find anger, or strong reactions, the necessary energy kick for writing. Possibly because I never directly write about myself, finding the personal lyric embarrassing (as attempted by me).

I'm surprised with what comes out. It's an unconscious alter-ego—which is why I use so many monologues. And I never censor for content. Of course, I edit for flow, rhythm, coherency of images and phasing of the poem's dynamics. That last, most of all.

I'll discuss this later, but I feel there are so many "unsaids" nowadays, and have always felt compelled to say them. I also like attacking myself in writing. However, I always try to get an element of release into the poems—especially in the most extreme stuff. Moments of stillness.

As an overview, I just don't engage with the saintly persona so many poets portray—especially how well adjusted and poetical their reactions are. Always available to flaunt their sensitive feelings.

The other point is, I'm always trying to use humour—but not in a surrealistic way, rather through grotesque satire or hyper-realism—moving through exaggeration, into possible delirium. The febrile state I like is most often initiated by anger; but I hope it is then cooled enough, transformed enough, to be readable.

I'd always assumed that your poetry was quite ironic, quoting what would normally be perceived as right wing views for the sake of dismissing or questioning them, but recently I've seen some blog entries which suggest you are quite conservative. Is this true?

In the arts, anyone of a non-left outlook has to justify themselves, because it just seems so unusual. And my responses are pushed to extremes, ironically or grotesquely, to get maximum energy and development from them. Above all else, that's what I want from writing—and something which wakes me up. But I'm not trying to "send up" right-wing views. That's for cringingly unfunny Radio 4 "satire".

I'm not aligned party politically, but very anti-left; remember, they are the establishment, socially and—especially—culturally. The latest shibboleth is multiculturalism and "equality"—preaching diversity yet incapable of accepting alternative views. And widening the gap between privileged and underprivileged.

The poetry world is mostly left/liberal—and pretty much unquestioningly so. Why? Huge numbers of the population aren't, whatever the BBC likes to pretend. Of course, they are easily dismissed as mindless "*Daily Mail/Sun*" readers. But it's not that simple.

In the recent exchange you allude to, on *Poets on Fire*, I was put in the dock for avowedly stating my dislike of the Left's damaging "diversity" agenda: did I refuse to acknowledge the existence of racism etc. Loaded questioning, of the "when did you stop beating your wife?" type. Hysterical and juvenile. I was clearly dealing with a fanatic, but the approach was fascinating—demanding I prove my worthiness, constantly misquoting—or rather creatively interpreting—what I said. With the word "racist" itching for deployment.

Teaching in a tough comprehensive, I don't need lectures on diversity, working as I do with some highly disadvantaged individuals, and seeing first hand the sort of society the left liberals have created. Disadvantaged not least by the blindly programmatic thinking of such *bien pensants*.

So, I am unashamedly not of the left-utopian outlook. I detest their lazy moral posturing, the solipsistic need for moral superiority—with little concern for the effects of their self-indulgence. Looking over the horrific catalogue of left-authoritarian mass murder and misery (or more recently, the disastrous trashing of our economy) I can't see how anyone takes them seriously. The asymmetry with atrocities/mistakes on the right is breathtaking.

My student political experiences (early 1980s Oxford) are probably responsible—incidentally, when people like Edward "Ed" Balls were there. Not a peep about the Soviet Union's Gulag and psychiatric wards—still in full swing. I especially loathe Marxist academics—how they prevaricate and fudge, how Stalinist apologists are rarely attacked, in the way that Nazi sympathisers (rightly) were.

This is covered in the sequence *Gib/Supplicants for the Emperor/House of Steam/House of Terror*—originally published in Luke Kennard's *Popularity Contest* and the American magazine *Vox*, back in 2004. I reject the idea that the Left's intentions are always good, let alone the outcomes. Anyone who reads Marx and Lenin will find violence is worshipped and regarded as essential.

But I'm aware my reactions are likely to get me into trouble, or at least be unpublished. And anyway, I want to parody and undermine my views. I'm half-aware that my approach seems nuts—in fact I like it to be. Because it's not meant to be a coherent philosophy—more a way to write.

Getting back to poetry, which is all I actually care about in this context, I associate this one sided discourse with the preachy lyrical anecdote—the ghastly mood music of the left-liberals. Ironic that this anecdotage is a conservative type of writing—but many experimental writers aren't on the left. Eliot, Pound, Céline, Kipling (in stories like 'Wireless' or 'Mrs Bathurst'), Wyndham Lewis, Henry Miller, Burroughs.

Also, I can't stand saintly lyrical perfection, of the type exemplified by Heaney or Su Tenderdrake. Thankfully, there's been some recent brilliant debunking of Heaney in *Jacket*—what a terrifyingly dull writer he is. I loathe how Heaney has used classical Greek literature to bolster his already enormous ego. And his absurd essay 'Dylan the durable?' Nothing by him even approaches Thomas.

I'm half-Greek. But also passionately and unashamedly English, it's just I lack the cringing attitude to supposed cosmopolitanism; I'm utterly unworried about appearing a "little Englander". And I hate all that mythical Irish bardic nonsense. I agree with The Crow's landlord in *Withnail and I*.

So are your poems partly an attempt to address what might be seen as a left wing or liberal discourse in contemporary poetry?

I'm trying to *use* the current discourse, in a reactive but creative way. But also just surfing the energies, allowing the monsters (on all sides) to surface. I've no interest in provoking political responses though, other than feelings of unease. I also couldn't care less whether people "agree" with me. That's meaningless, in creative work.

Is this perhaps why—like many others—you don't seem part of any real or imaginary school of poetry?

I think these are inherently corrupt and corrupting. All I've ever done is asked for blurbs, from people who've published me. That seems ethical. And most of the time, I don't know what to make of my own stuff, so I'd be clueless about being in any school or movement.

Slowly and selectively though, I've built up poetry contacts—you for example—but only via submissions or serious correspondence about work. I wouldn't know you, if we passed in the street.

My BlazeVox book came about from a poetry submission, to their brilliant online magazine. But looking at some of the brilliant people they publish—Anne Waldman and Daniel Borzutzky for example—I'm really chuffed.

I know many take this low-key approach—but plenty of others don't. All sorts of guff is spouted about the social nature of writing, the need for co-operation, Facebook, Twittering, etc. It's simply a justification for log rolling—posting cheesy comments on Facebook, endlessly affirming each other, posting "smileys" and saying hello/happy birthday to total strangers. Yeuch.

For understandable reasons (like paying the bills) some UK publishers are fixated on this aspect, but it all seems very incestuous and toe curling. What I also resent is the idea that this relentless promotion validates work—almost via a perverted version of the intelligent market idea. Luckily, the internet can free writers from this nonsense, allowing them access to very rich material (and other publishers) around the world.

Also, a self-congratulatory London grouping of *arrivistes* has arisen, prattling on about the place and its multicultural energies, sounding like some New Labour propaganda unit.

Maybe that's unfair—I don't care. I was born in London and lived/worked there for years—love the city, but hate this embarrassingly star-struck aspect. Anyone who knows this country realises that the real interest and action is in the motorway/retail world of Ballard or Sinclair (at times)—Bicester Village and Homebase.

Meanwhile, back in London, figures like Roddy Lumsden patrol the "scene", twitching and sniffing out the nay-sayers—with increasing desperation. It's worrying that his writing seems so gimmicky and weak—nothing like good enough to justify a supposedly central role. The results, as seen in *Identity Parade*, are mostly appalling. And the photos! Like a 1980s student ragmag.

By necessity, he works through a climate of patronage and intimidation—though it's not actually clear what there is to be frightened of. But I do remember him pathetically threatening violence to the people at the magazine *Thumbscrew*, years ago. For goodness sake, maybe Gordon Brown could have taken Lumsden back up with him? I'd have thought it's the least he could have done.

Pity we poor English, with these grotesque Caledonian overlords. Freeeeeeedom! How I cheer at the end of *Braveheart*—aren't you supposed to?

Your poems explore a half-submerged violence, some kind of resistance to corporate life, surveillance and expected normality. Would you like to respond to that?

I think our normalising left liberals are storing up violence—in fact, provoking it. They don't know—and actively despise—their own country, especially England. Witness Brown on walkabout, or Jacqui Smith, plus armed response unit, getting a kebab in Peckham. Also their deliberate use of immigration as a political and economic weapon.

I worked in the corporate world for years, as a commercial negotiator. A violent and brutal environment. It was massively inspiring—I suppose I wrote as a way of freeing myself. Often *at* work—with the delicious risk of discovery… maybe that feeds into my stuff on surveillance.

Brains Scream at Night *reads as a kind of selected poems, with sequences and individual poems many of us will have already read gathered up. Is this fair, or has there always been a bigger concept in your head?*

It does collect some published work from all over the place, but we (myself and editor Geoffrey Gatza) planned the sequencing—the way it's arranged in seven sections based on forms and themes—as carefully as possible. It's very sequence and character driven—I love narrative poetry—but meant to show a transition. The last part (*The Chronicles of Dave Turnip*) is not monologue based, but inspired by different types of syllable/stress counts and elliptical forms. Also written to be as cold and image based as possible. Throughout, my underlying concepts are as discussed above.

My first collection *Broadsheet Asphyxia* (Original Plus, 2003) uses less sequences but still covers this territory. I guess we all have our obsessions; I certainly see it all as a project.

What are you influences? How do you go about writing?

Orwell was my first great love. Then Waugh and Greene.

Original poetry influences were Shelley, Coleridge, Browning, Eliot, Pound, Dylan Thomas, Rosemary Tonks, Roy Fisher. The latter is a huge moral inspiration, for his integrity. I wrote him a gauche fan letter in 1999, and then corresponded, on and off about his work.

More recently Ken Smith, John Barnie, Ashbery, Ginsberg, Peter Reading. Most recently—through BlazeVox—writers like Daniel Borzutzky and Aaron Belz. I also find David Mamet and Pinter very inspiring.

Prose writers like Céline, Genet and Bolaño. Especially Céline—such a genius with imprecation. Also Wilkie Collins, Conan Doyle, Dostoyevsky, Kafka, Kipling, Maugham, Patricia Highsmith, Iain Sinclair.

I also find film massively inspiring, especially stuff like the Coens or *The Wages of Fear* and also the Bourne films. Some of the images for 'Turnip in Love' are from that haunting motorway scene, where he's driving with the girl.

I wait to be provoked before writing. I also need to feel pressured, short of time—almost on the run. The stresses and joys of teaching are in some ways inspiring, but the responsibility most definitely is not; so maybe reacting against that is.

And how did you first get into poetry?

I started writing poetry age 15 (1979)—sub-Eliot stuff. Then kept at it, in secret, until trying to get stuff published in about 2000. I joined a local Oxford poetry group in 1998—most there detested me, and vice versa, but I made two amazing poetry friends. And got involved in organizing some readings of poets I revere—e.g. Roy Fisher, David Harsent, Ken Smith, Martin Stannard, John Barnie.

Incidentally, I think my fake dissident approach may be due to the fact that I read Chemistry at Oxford—and then did a doctorate there, in Physical Chemistry ('Some studies in Infrared Multiple Photon Excitations')—using IR lasers to initiate reactions, then studying the fragments with UV/visible lasers. Although I did well at this (First, etc.) I also felt I was doing totally the wrong thing. I'd got channelled down the Oxbridge route—entrance exam, Sciences etc. I felt trapped and false, leading a double life. Looking back, writing allowed me a form of re-birth.

So now I teach English, at a secondary school! My proudest achievement is getting a student into Oxford, to read English, two years ago.

What are you working on at the moment?

I'm writing a sequence set in Amalfi, about a fake writer-in-residence; obsessed with "the romance of crime", using it to try and give some spice to his cushioned position.

Thanks for your interest.

[*Stride* 2010]

The Power of Having Fun

AN INTERVIEW WITH STEVE SPENCE

RUPERT LOYDELL: *Pirates! Why the fascination with these nautical miscreants?*

STEVE SPENCE: What an interesting question! To which there is more than one answer, I guess. There are two poems in *A Curious Shipwreck* which were written more than ten years before the rest. One of these, 'Pirates', is probably the starting point for the collection and came about as a result of a dream I had which related, somewhat obliquely I recall, to a primary school reading book about pirates. I think there were four pirate captains and each had a colour—red, blue, yellow and green. This gave me the structure for my poem, which featured six pirates, each having a colour and a stanza to himself. It's a prose poem and was written very quickly, using word/idea association and anything that came into my head as I was writing, very different from the construction of the bulk of the work in *Shipwreck*. There are around half a dozen pieces in the book which were written, more or less, in this manner, the rest being constructed—to a large extent—by montage techniques, utilising a wide range of found materials (including a couple of short pieces of fiction of "my own" which I consequently cut-up) as well as material I invented along the way.

I'm wandering from the point though. I guess that I had it in mind to write a series of poems on the theme of pirates based on that original piece but it never really came to anything until, that is, I started doing the M.A. in Creative Writing in 2006. The opportunity to do this course at the University of Plymouth turned out to be really important for me as I had to focus intensely over a relatively short period and became much more productive as a result. I had to put a book of poems together from scratch in a four month period through the summer of 2007. I decided to have a go at resuscitating the pirate theme—necessity *is* the mother of invention!—and my early attempts of around half a dozen more-or-less mainstream narrative poems were pretty dull. I needed a method or I obviously wasn't going to see the project through. I'd written a few pieces which were partly collaged material but having Tony Lopez as my tutor for the dissertation turned into a godsend as his working methods meant that he was very supportive to the approach. You could even say that he encouraged the project into being. Once I'd got going I found the whole process great fun: gathering materials in the mornings usually and spending the afternoons trying to piece things together so that they worked, either as texture or as non-sequitur or as forming some kind of coherent sense amid the "nonsense". I produced around two thirds of the material that now exists as *A Curious Shipwreck* during that period.

I wouldn't say that I had a *fascination* with pirates, other than the usual childhood interest but it's become increasingly obvious to me that The Pirate is a very useful metaphor for a lot of the stuff that's been going on in the world recently. What did fascinate me as I read more deeply into the subject, is the way in which the contradiction at the heart of piracy—between collective action and individualist "free-market" economics, allied to its lawless, outsider designation (although never forget that Drake's privateers were "legalised pirates")—provides an intriguing base for an exploration of contemporary issues, distanced through an already thoroughly romanticised popular history. Great material for poetry and that's before you even begin thinking about vocabulary and playing with the clichés.

Apart from having fun, what are you doing with these poems? What would you expect readers to come away with?

Well, I wouldn't underestimate the power of having fun, for a start. The enjoyment I got from the process of producing those poems was an important part of their meaning and surely this filters through to the reader in some form. I hope so, anyway because the last thing I want to be doing is labouring over material which turns out to be dull and dusty, bored and boring! That said there is clearly a satirical impulse behind these poems. The theme of Piracy creates a kind of framework in which to operate and I've already suggested that it seems to be quite an appropriate theme for the times we live in. Now I don't want to get all political about this but I guess a big part of my problem with writer's block (does it exist!) over the past few years has been my inability to find a way of producing poetry which is in some sense political—or at least engaging with "issues"—in a manner which avoids being didactic and boring or ranty and angry. Okay, I write the odd rant and I guess the ones that actually work are quite funny but it seems quite difficult, these days, to produce poetry which has a political dimension without either seeming incredibly angry all the time, or seeming politically correct in a po-faced manner or, more usually, simply seeming redundant and "un-cool". I don't mind being un-cool, in fact I quite relish the thought, but boring…! that's another thing altogether. There are writers or "models" I admire and have been influenced by—from Barry MacSweeney and Ken Smith (in *Fox Running*), through Bill Herbert, Gordon Wardman, Tom Leonard, John Hartley Williams, Peter Finch and Kelvin Corcoran, for example—as well as Robert Sheppard and Tony Lopez, whose work with montage and sampling news reportage has been influential—but I guess that I'm still learning and trying to forge my own way through and we'll have to see where that takes me next. As far as readers are concerned I can only hope, above all, that the work is entertaining in some sense as well as providing provocation and perhaps, at times bewilderment. I've learnt a lot from work that I've initially been bewildered by but I guess you've got to find enough interest and curiosity in the material to want to delve beneath your first impressions.

How did Alice get into the mix?

One of the source materials for *A Curious Shipwreck*, believe it or not, was *Alice in Wonderland*. I nicked a line or two for the poems but the figure of Alice began to appear intermittently throughout the text and particularly in some of the poems I wrote later which appear, perhaps confusingly, earlier in the book. Two people have said to me since the publication of the book that I should have used Alice more, as a predominant motif, throughout the collection, and I think they may have a point. Certainly there is a liveliness in that group of poems, they appear less abstract, perhaps, and there is a convivial yet argumentative aspect which I could have developed more. I still have masses of material left over from that project but I'm not sure the world could handle another book of "Pirate Poems" from Spence. How egotistical is that!

Your collages are apparently left quite raw. Is knowing how these poems are made an important part of the reading experience? Are you ever tempted to smooth out the syntax, tense and grammar?

That's a tricky question to answer. I guess it's partly true that the rawness you allude to is at least partly down to the fact that producing this collection has been part of a learning process. I wouldn't want to deny that and some of the current material I've been working on (another project) has perhaps ironed out some of the more abrupt juxtapositions and made the work seem smoother and more seamless. Then again, I quite like abrupt juxtapositions too and some of the funnier "episodes" in *Shipwreck* come about (I think) when the non-sequiturs are both ludicrously inappropriate (mad) and obscurely weird. I'll give you a short example to try and justify that point:

> "Are you a book detective or a pirate?" Next to
> join the frenzy are the clerks. On the other hand,
> you could spend a lifetime researching the
> physiology of walking, or just take to the high seas.
>   (from 'Romeo & Ethel—the pirate's daughter')

That still makes me laugh. I could try and explain it away by giving you the sources (I can't just now recall the origin of the last sentence though I suspect it has two areas of reference) but I think that would miss the point. André Breton said somewhere—and this will be a rough paraphrase because (huh) I can't recall where—that when you appropriate material and reintegrate it into a different context you always get something more interesting than you'd come up with on your own. Now, I don't *necessarily* agree with that but a big part of the process of composition is to do with making choices and when you have a vast well from which to draw your material the question of choosing becomes an even more crucial part of the process. I guess there are (still) people out there who consider this way of working to be "false" in some way, or cheating, or "not real", or "inauthentic", to which I can only respond by saying look at the history of the visual arts over the last century, particularly film. Collage and montage are taken for granted as a means of working within the cinema, it's a central part of the grammar of film, and is commonly accepted by most people because it *appears* to be as *natural* as breathing. Deconstruction can be a cruel business but revealing the methods is a very necessary part of a self-reflective process, even if you then learn to perform your art in the manner of riding a bicycle—not by thinking about it but by doing it! I guess that I would hope that anyone reading these poems would have some idea of how they were put together but perhaps I shouldn't assume that. Nathan Thompson pointed out in his very generous review on the *Stride* site (thanks, Nathan) that:

> the syntax makes sense, and your brain is deceived into believing
> all is well, then you stop to think and realise you've no idea what
> is going on. It's a poetry deliberately designed to wrong-foot you,
> to trick you out of trusting language…

Steve Spence   183

I like that. It *is* a destabilising mode of writing and I take on board the implications of that, in the sense that there is an underlying "critical" or "political" aim but I don't think that has to mean the writing has to be either po-faced or hopelessly difficult. Surely re-making the world is a necessary part of artistic endeavour and you can question things without being forever puritanical about it. How's that for an A-Level philosophy question! I would certainly agree that there are points in *Shipwreck* where the joins show and where it might be better if they didn't. I'm sure the process will improve but I wouldn't want to iron out all the rough edges....!

Tell us about your poetical journey towards becoming a textural plunderer?

Mmm. It's probably a natural progression from picking out odd lines from existing texts (whether fiction, news items, history, science, economics, cookery, writing on music or even advertising materials) or snippets of overheard conversation, to a more systematic use of this method. It was certainly the necessity of producing a large amount of material in a relatively short time that made me investigate the process more seriously while I was doing the M.A. Prior to this, as I've already said, there were lengthy periods when I felt blocked but in any case my output rate was pretty low compared to where I am now and possibly had an air of preciousness about it, though I don't think that's how I perceived it at the time. The poems I was writing before I started work on the book were mainly more compressed than those I produce now and there's an aspect of that which I'd like to recapture and develop at some point. Having for once an overall theme for a group of poems and seeing the completion of a book as a project in itself tends to give you both a clear goal and a set of borders within which to work. I see the process of working with existing materials in a big way as an extension of how I'd sometimes worked before. Then it was simply a matter of deciding what materials to use and apart from the obvious trick of working with writing relating to seafaring and to piracy I was determined to bring in a wide range of stuff, partly to avoid the obvious clichés but also to make the writing as strange (and perhaps *estranged*) as I possibly could. I wanted the book to be an entertainment but one which didn't necessarily come too easily—it needed to be surprising and to contain the unexpected and to be puzzling to boot. I took material from films and from the radio as well as from newspapers and journals but mainly from books in a wide range of topics and styles. Science, economics, history, fiction, fashion and theory were all areas of writing from which I plundered, sometimes as a direct steal (I assume that's what you mean when

Steve Spence

you talk about the "raw") but often mucking around with the sentences/ snippets in various ways, adding or changing words, bringing pirates into the mix quite overtly and by running different sentences together to create something strange and unexpected. Nathan Thompson, in his review of the book mentions the term flarf (I had to google that one) which refers to a ten-year-old American group who use the internet to randomly bring together different texts, often with a scatological or shocking aim but also as an anti-aesthetic aesthetic, at least that's how I understand the term. Now, I think my work is perhaps (hopefully) more concerned with some notion of beauty or "textural pleasure" than the term flarf implies but I also defend its critical or de-familiarising function and I think the two aims can run together. Tony Lopez's work, for example, certainly seems to feature both these aspects.

Is the book a sequence or just a number of poems working with the same idea or on the same theme?

Well, it's obviously the overall theme of "piracy" which holds the collection together, both in the sense of piracy as subject and in terms of piracy or plunder as a method of construction. Within that structure I think there are several groups of poems which perhaps have a distinctive form or topic-within-a-topic—for example, the fourteen poems where Alice features as a major device/participant. I've had to cut out a lot of material along the way so the overall form of the book is an attempt to bring together the best of the material, which was written in bursts with occasional time-lapses between. The five poems which were essentially written in a more stream-of-consciousness mode—including the tribute to George Melly, 'Revolt into Style and On the Hoe' (the first to be written and more or less adapted to fit the book) are included because I think they add variety and a more spontaneous energy to the whole. I think there may in fact be a *series* of sequences within the book, representing attempts to diverge and try out different things. The final poem in the book (not the final one to be written but the last I produced before completing the M.A. thesis)—'The Empire of Fear', still stands for me as one of the most interesting and exploratory pieces to be included. I think by this point I'd developed a way of working with montaged material that became more spontaneous and creative. This is difficult to describe as a process but it may be worth attempting, even if in a tentative and faltering manner. I was taking more risks with "inventing on the spot" and merging the collected materials with more spontaneous thoughts and adaptations which seemed to make the piece flow more easily. It was certainly great fun to write—I was working at some speed and in a kind of heightened state which usually only happens to me when I'm producing an improvised rant (on the rare occasions it works effectively) and the experience of composition felt like pure pleasure. I had a break from those poems after completing 'Empire of Fear' but I sort of wish I'd just kept going because I think I'd got into a flow and had learned how to work that material more effectively, riffing more easily and with the confidence which comes with a degree of build-up and familiarity with the process. I still think it's the most interesting piece in the collection. As I've said earlier I think the overall organisation of the book is far from perfect and if I was starting again from scratch I'd probably do it very differently but that's all part of the learning curve.

Do you write other sorts of poems? What are you working on at the moment?

I've just pretty much completed a new collection—shorter, 60 odd poems but with each poem fitting on a page, different format but using similar procedures of composition. There is no overall theme but there are a number of topics which recur or are reprised throughout the collection. Clouds feature quite heavily, for example. I'm probably going to call it *Does Your English Let you Down?* the title of one of the poems you recently posted on the Stride site. I think I've got someone interested in publishing it but nothing has been finalised yet. I continued to work in this manner partly because I wanted to see if I could keep it going and develop the processes but also because of a fear that I might dry up. Yes, I do write other sorts of poem and now that the new project is more or less complete I want to get back to trying to produce some more spontaneous material. I've got around 40 pages of poetry—the best of the stuff I've written over the past fifteen years or so—which I'd like to get published in book form at some point but I need to be producing new work to add to the mix. I'm also keen to explore the performance end of the process and perhaps simplify or expand on the more rhythmic aspect of my earlier work. I've been listening, in particular, to John Agard and Bill Herbert reading their work recently and both are fantastic live readers, using musical idioms in which to write and perform. I'd like to try something more along those lines but it remains to be seen whether I have the necessary skills for that sort of refinement, which looks and sounds much easier than I know it to be. I also did a couple of readings/performances with some Jazz musicians several years back, including the composer/improviser Sam Richards, which was great fun and confidence boosting, something I'd certainly like to try again.

I'd like to add something here about the importance of writing groups in relation to the fostering of creativity, particularly if you happen to hit on a really good one. When I got involved in The Plymouth Language Club, or the Poetry Exchange, as I think it was then called, in the early to mid-90s, it was mainly run along the lines of a very open-ended workshop event, where writers came to read their material and have it commented on. I'd been involved with groups before, in Swindon and Cambridge, mainly, but had never found them very useful although that may have had something to do with me not being "hungry" enough at the time. By the time I turned up in Plymouth, I was very open to what was going on and through my involvement with *Terrible Work* and the members of the Poetry Exchange and the Language Club I discovered that there were a lot of interesting things happening in the region and within the small presses more generally. It got me writing seriously at long last and also helping to promote readings again which is something I'd had a fair bit of experience of in the past. My initial period of late development as a writer was slow but I improved and was taking in a wide variety of influence both through the group and via a wider access to publishing through the small press. This was all before the internet kicked in big-time. That and the opportunities created by doing the M.A. have moved things on again and I now find myself in the position of thinking about the next book rather than the next poem (!) which is all very strange but exciting.

[*Stride*, 2010]

Even the Bad Times are Good

RUPERT LOYDELL & ROBERT SHEPPARD

RUPERT LOYDELL: I've (finally) re-read When Bad Times Made for Good Poetry *and if you're still up for it, perhaps we can start a conversation-cum-interview about some of the issues it does and doesn't raise?*

ROBERT SHEPPARD: Of course, although the issues it doesn't raise might be either for another day, another book, or another writer!

Firstly, I wanted to ask if you would consider the "episodes" in your book the most important episodes in 'the history of the poetics of innovation' as your subtitle suggests, or simply episodes you were personally involved or aware of at the time?

The book is episodic in structure, in that it is a miscellany of previously published and unpublished pieces, and that is one meaning of the word (which avoids a sequentially oriented term such as "chapter" or one like "article" which implies complete narrative discontinuity). I try to avoid locutions like "the most important" because to truly make such a claim requires what we used to call "perfect knowledge" in A-Level Economics. In short, the episodes are various in scope. I write about Tom Raworth, Allen Fisher and Maggie O'Sullivan because they are extraordinary writers and deserve whatever elucidation I can offer to assist other readers to approach their difficulties of text and poetics. Iain Sinclair is culturally visible and requires critical mediation. There are other episodes—the long one on the "creative environment" of London in the mid-1980s, the one on the Poetry Society's manifesto, and the account of the circumstances of Ken Edwards' talk 'The WE Expression'—in which I hope I bring to readers who weren't there a sense of what it was like to be a part of a particular field of literary production, to use the sociological language I utilise in the book, a field which was crossed by both important figures (as writers, publishers, practitioners of poetics), and lesser-known characters. In fact, one of the things that surprised me in writing the piece that documents Bob Cobbing's London creative environment, Writers Forum, New River Project,—I'd made a decision to account for all the named agents in detailed footnotes—is how many of the people around at that time—poets, musicians, actors and others—have had distinguished careers since. Very few people simply went off the radar, though some changed course. I abandoned academic protocol and went personal (using diary fragments, etc.) because I felt that was the best way. A couple of thoughts on that: I wish I'd kept accurate notes at the time. Secondly: I was writing *The Given* at the same time, my attempt at an anti-autobiography, parts of which cover the same years, so I was awash with episodic memory.

I understand poetics is not a term only to do with poetry, but I wonder if you would concede that Iain Sinclair's importance to poetics, and indeed as a writer is more to do with his prose [although this obviously blurs into prose poetry at times] and as an editor and enabler?

I think that's true, but before *White Chappell, Scarlet Tracings* poetry was his main occupation, which is why I look at the poems of the early 1980s in the book: that extraordinary period when he published in editions of less than 20; the poems seem to form themselves from the wounds of Thatcherism! The second essay on Sinclair deals with the documentary prose, particularly the parts where he deals with the poetry world. I think his mythologising of individuals within this (which I criticise both here and in my book Iain Sinclair) is one reason why I felt drawn to try to be as inclusive as possible about the creative environments I witnessed myself. Indeed, you raise the word "poetics", which is a theme of many of the episodes. By poetics I mean the speculative writerly discourse, baggy and unruly, that writers use to conceptualise their past, present and (most importantly) future writings. It's the heart of my teaching and the life-force of my own writing. And I think Sinclair's failure to describe poetics (his own or others') in favour of impressionistic character-studies, is regrettable. I recognise the power of his writing: after all, I took the title of the book from one of his poems of the early 1980s. I recognise my complicity in this, too; I've used a quote of his that mythologises me a bit as a blurb for *Berlin Bursts*, the poetry book that was published simultaneously with *Bad Times* by Shearsman! Liverpool hasn't noticed me! But I'm bigger than Ringo!

Conductors of Chaos in many ways seemed a summary of something gone and dealt with. Would you agree that it wasn't a particularly readable or enjoyable book, more a thorn in the side of mainstream poetry, a kind of agent provocateur?

Seemed? You mean at the time, 1996? It summarised a little (there were those excerpts from neglected modernists). Isn't this Sinclair as "enabler"? All anthologies play catch up. Perhaps a tangent: Sinclair gets rolled out to talk about the poetry scene sometimes, such as on a recent BBC radio programme on Bob Cobbing, but it is interesting how little I ever came across him in that environment. He wasn't an eye/ear witness often. In fact, given that, it is surprising that he found new voices such as Caroline Bergvall or Aaron Williamson for that anthology; their appearance probably owes to Catling's influence. It's quite readable. Only recently has Sinclair perceived the importance of Ken Edwards (one of Sinclair's books of the year) or John Seed (included in *City of Disappearances*), for example, both mentioned in my book (indeed, both dedicatees of it: I dedicate it to the few people who turned up to my SubVoicive reading in December 1985! The first work after my post-modernist breakthrough! Fit though few.) Sinclair is both sustained and handicapped by his practice of walking out into the culture (literally, often) to see what he finds.

My personal experience of '70s and early '80s London and poetry is very different to the world discussed and described in your book. Did you consider writing more of a survey of innovative poetries at the time?

Last point first. My previous volume *The Poetry of Saying* attempted an historical academic account of some innovative practices (defined technically, linguistically and ethically) whereas *Bad Times* approaches this episodically (and also is more aimed at the poetry "scene" itself than at university library shelves where the earlier book languishes). There is some (deliberate) overlap. I can only do what I can do. There are writers I admire but about whom I could say nothing very useful. All that stuff I read in translation, for instance. At one time I might have attempted a "survey"; such a venture seems to me fit for an edited volume by many hands these days. Reading Andrew Duncan puts me off panoptic narratives. My only response to your experience is: write your own account. Perhaps what's needed is: Maximum Accounts: Minimum Surveys (to paraphrase Emperor Rosko on Radio Luxembourg French in the late 1960s). I've just read both Pasternak's *Safe Conduct* and Shklovsky's *Mayakovsky and his Circle* (for different reasons, and not thinking of them together) and was fascinated by the overlap, and the one convergence when both writers meet over the corpse of their mutual friend, about whom they held differing, but reverent, views.

I came to poetry through the likes of Ted Hughes' Crow sequence (which I saw him read in Hammersmith, the same week as Ivor Cutler performed there!) and picking up remaindered anthologies and early editions of Slow Dancer magazine in an Oxford Street bookshop. Gavin Selerie's Azimuth, which I bought in the Riverside Studios bookshop, was very important to me; so was seeing Peter Redgrove and others read in Holland Park, and Tom Pickard and Robert Creeley at Riverside Studios.

In retrospect, I think there's an argument that innovative poetries were just as dependent on some of these other strands of poetry and other activities such as improvised and other performances at the London Musicians' Collective premises, zine culture (perhaps with a nod to Tom Vague and the Rough Trade shops), performance poetry descending from the likes of both Adrian Mitchell and the Liverpool Poets but also reggae and dub (which then mutates into rap) centred perhaps in Notting Hill and Brixton. I might add post-punk in general, which for my money actually did something lyrically and musically with some of the possibilities punk offered, more mainstream poets such as Ken Smith, and the political sloganeering and pamphleteering (which I regard as really interesting textual and publishing activities) of Crass and similar politically motivated groups within the anarchist and post-punk world.

This might not be your London, and your book couldn't possibly have included all of my list, but I wondered if you'd care to comment? Might the rhizomean idea that you used in Twentieth Century Blues *be an appropriate model when considering the networks of poetic innovation?*

See? You're starting to offer your account, geographically to the west of where I was, and maybe slightly earlier or more extensive in time. (I'm not a Londoner; lived there 1982-1997.) What is interesting is not the divergence but its opposite: Gavin Selerie, the musicians of the LMC, Pickard and Creeley, these cross the accounts I've put together. *Slow Dancer* I remember well, Ken Smith I knew later, oddly, and he didn't seem "mainstream" in the early '80s. I ought to write on him; he's nearly been forgotten (as he feared at the time, I'm told). I saw (and at the time admired) Peter Redgrove, actually reading at the Poetry Society at what must have been the time of the biggest turmoil. I was too shy to approach him, but stayed (at the bar) talking to Cobbing and Upton. There was a factional friction in the room I didn't understand (and I hope Redgrove didn't either). Again, I wish I'd kept detailed accounts, as perhaps you have. Was this the night I picked up/was picked up by a drunk woman on Earl's Court station who'd been to a party thrown by the Heavy Metal Kids, and we returned to her flat to find it full of dope-smoking heads? (I made my retreat hastily and caught the Brighton train, then running all night.) Punk passed me by. I was busy (still) reading Marcuse's 'Essay on Liberation'.

Rhizomatic criticism? Yes, indeed, if it were possible. Not so much rhizomatic as prismatic. Again, I think multiple views are needed. I've talked to Robert Hampson about this, and I think we concluded a web resource would be ideal to capture these histories and memories. Gavin Selerie is alert to the need to document the London scene beyond my parameters—and we've corresponded and chatted about this. He has images, too, as does Paul A. Green. Geraldine Monk sent me other photos taken on the same day as the cover image of Cobbing and O'Sullivan at the LMC. It's different today. I was talking about this to Tim Atkins who was reading at Edge Hill the day before yesterday. You can't read in public these days without being recorded. Back then, people couldn't afford film for cameras. Tape recorders broke and nobody could fix them.

I've asked you and others this question before, but I'm going to ask it again: Why on earth was so much energy spent trying to subvert and claim The Poetry Society for innovative poetries? Why expect an establishment mainstream group to be doing anything interesting and worthwhile? Wouldn't it have been easier to leave well alone and get on with it elsewhere, perhaps supporting some of the alternative bookshops and organisations that could have done with audiences and sales of books and refreshments? Was there any logic to trying to reposition both the Society and experimental poetry in the way that was attempted?

No, you've not asked me quite this question before, but it's an interesting one. Given the alternative society/ies documented in *Bomb Culture* and elsewhere, why did they bother? There must have been a logic, but what was it? The answer has to lie in looking carefully at the contemporary situation. Our view is misted by the failure of events at Earl's Court, but what if they'd succeeded? In my short story writing phase a few years ago I considered writing an alternative history in which radical poetry is culturally validated: I plotted a scene in which Lawrence Upton is discovered in a hammock in the high rise studios-cum-offices of the Institute of Advanced Poetics. (He'd recognise the comic allusion to his visit to Sweden in the 1970s when he discovered a very comfortably funded avant-garde artist in a similar attitude, by the way!) Imagine if we'd treated Roy Fisher as well as we ought; he might have won the Nobel Prize alongside Tranströmer this year. They are very similar poets in many ways. Imagine!

The 1960s ended in or about 1973 or 1974, didn't they? I'm not thinking about *Dark Side of the Moon* or T-Rex but the buffers of the oil crisis of 1973. Again, the ravages of Thatcherism, or the faceless contempt of Cameron, mask the fact that something commonly perceptible was shifting economically at that point. Things looked a little meaner. That had effects. Fulcrum and other presses had folded, Better Books was gone, had been re-absorbed by Collins. Where else was there a premises to use with a fit for purpose performance space in London? Underground magazines folded, the alternative poetry magazines became little magazines again, purely literary. Here was a subsidised journal for the taking. The Society was less a mainstream institution at that time than a moribund shell. Some of these factors point to the narrowing of opportunities; others represent the sharpening of foci, as in the creative work of many of the participants at Earls Court. Perhaps both.

If we take Peter Barry's *Poetry Wars* as the data and speculate a little, we can see that the entryism at Earls Court was gradual and probably not premeditated, but there had been a growing movement towards consolidation via the Association of Little Presses which had been promoting independent publishing (or perhaps it's better to think of it as interdependent publishing, remembering tales of Raworth rushing round to literally borrow print from Asa Benveniste, for example!). ALP was particularly interested in schemes of distribution of poetry books; it's not hard to see that the Society could have potentially organised and funded this—and did, for a while. There was room for a print room that many presses could use, without having to borrow type! Poets Conference (an unofficial Trades Union), chiefly organised, like ALP, by Cobbing, kept poetry reading organisers on their toes. The Society administered the then-important Poetry Secretariats that ensured payment and subsidy for poetry reading, which might surprise younger poets used to door money (or less). Again, the attractions of Arts Council money are obvious, and the poets (rightly or wrongly) saw access to this as almost a right. Poets Conference voted Adrian Mitchell as their candidate for poet laureate and "conveners" Bob and George MacBeth were received gracefully by poetically-informed civil servants at Downing Street, Bob once told me. Receiving such a reception alone must have felt like being at the heart of things.

The Society was also national news. It was a NATIONAL poetry centre and they must have eyed it like freedom fighters coveting the radio station (which is not to pass over the premises' disrepair). One of the surprises about Peter's book is the extent of press coverage and publicity they were getting. They must have believed that if you have control of the content of the *Poetry Review* you could influence its already existing readership, and detourn poetry as a whole. (Today *Poetry Review* speciously calls itself THE "poetry journal of record".) You were potentially breaking out of the narrowing circle of the underground into the mainstream, which you would then transform by education, faster than by other means. (In fact, subscribers unsubscribed, as we say today.) This was an era in which Cobbing, for one, was working a lot in schools. School textbooks and anthologies carried poems by Cobbing, Harwood, Paul Evans, etc., so there were encouraging signs in the culture at large. The Education Office of the Society might have seemed a body worth infiltrating. The early seventies must have seemed like a tipping point. Added to that, self-delusion and a few pints in the bar (another pull, it could stay open all night if need be!) and they were onto a winner, but they were caught off-guard by events. Rather than tell that story again, I concentrate in my piece in *Bad Times* on the forgotten, unreleased manifesto, which is unashamedly utopian in its desire for imaginative thinking to spread right through society, in its belief that poetry is one instrument of society's liberation. The "logic to the attempted repositioning", to use your phrase, Rupert, is contained in this manifesto (mainly the work of Nuttall I'd guess, and reprinted entire in Peter Barry's book). They were talking to the nation (they thought). Or they could have been. If Kenneth Goldsmith can read in the White House, then Cobbing could have read at Number 10. Actually, when he performed before Edward Heath at a concert he turned his back on him. Most of these people could not have maintained the kinds of necessary bureaucratic compromises learned by other kinds of arts organisers.

In short: this must have felt like a period of narrowing opportunity, coupled with perceptibly emboldened ambition and the Poetry Society would have seemed replete with resources, physical and financial to effect large-scale societal change, not just in poetry.

Of course, you're right about my point of view being influenced by now, but to me the '70s was about a repositioning of power, not attempts to take over. Of course some bands signed up to EMI, but at the time after punk there genuinely were new record labels springing up. It seemed to me the fruition of the more idealistic '60s, a time when utopian vision had to deal with business in some way; there was— finally!—an understanding that books and records didn't magically appear in the ether, they were produced objects that had to be distributed and sold. Of course, Oz, International Times and many other magazines had set a precedent. To me, coming late to the small press party, there was still a euphoria in the air; possibilities were available—Stride itself was started as a result of that, and Stride cassettes was part of the DIY cassette scene that happened in the early 80s, an early way of cheap music and poetry distribution.

Wasn't it also about storming the reality studios? Your 1970s are the punk late 1970s, when all of this was over (bar the final fighting). As I say in the book, I was lucky in catching some of the late euphoria myself when I was still quite young—I was 20 in 1975—and absorbed that DIY ethos well: in the 1970s I was publishing *1983*—the date sounded futuristic at the time, and nodded to Hendrix and Hugh Hopper!—a technologically up-to-date cassette tape magazine that published Harwood, Griffiths, Paul Evans and Stefan Themerson, among others, the latter an important figure in showing that innovation had a history (at the time I knew him I hadn't clocked he'd been a friend of Schwitters).

I guess my question arises out of genuine bemusement: why take over or subvert something when you can do it so much better yourself! The Poetry Society has always been London-centric, and its allegiances to arts council funding and the bigger poetry presses (through the Poetry Book Society) then and now mean it was unlikely to ally itself with experimental and alternative poetries. It was and is too invested in the mainstream. The best we can have hoped for might be the all-inclusive magazine editions that Robert Potts edited. I suspect many innovative poets remain resistant to this, as we both know many poets consider the way they write the only way to write! I've documented elsewhere my amazement at poets' abilities to discard the likes of Faber in one go, or whole poetic movements in a single statement. One hopes that there are more accepting and catholic critics and writers around nowadays, without wishing for uncritical readers and writers.

Very briefly (we must move on from this subject!) there was both the sense that new and independent things could happen within the society. Cobbing already owned the means of production for Writers Forum (the office duplicator) but other presses did make use of the print room (Bill Griffiths' Pirate Press, for example). Remember, the radical poets arrived one by one and I don't think they were conscious until it happened that they were taking it over. And they did for a while. The 'Manifesto' is catholic, recognising the varieties of contemporary poetry, though the *Poetry Review* didn't. You're right that a national centre should publish an all-inclusive review. Potts did, and what happened? He was replaced. It's no wonder innovative poets respond in the ways you suppose; "mainstream" poets do too. Mutual incomprehension. I am less likely to issue death-threats to the mainstream these days: I enjoyed doing so through my *New Statesman* reviews of the 1980s—but that seems a long time ago. Nowadays, I don't systematically study the "mainstream"; my last pronouncements were in *The Poetry of Saying* where I look at the rainbow alliances of millennial anthologies that declared all poetry wars over and everyone the winners: in a sociologically-defined catholicity that included (as far as I could see) representatives of most groupings, but not of what has come to be collected under that term "linguistically innovative".

Allen Fisher appears twice in your book, but despite much critical attention, his own public placement over the years as an artist, poet and educator, and the fairly recent publication of his major sequences, he is perhaps one of the most off-the-radar innovative poets in terms of the general public or poetry readers. Any ideas why this is? I personally find his poetry intriguing and musical, if not transparent in terms of "meaning" or "content". Does Allen prefer being a cult author do you think?

No, he's not a cult author, by my understanding: that would entail a following of hip insiders deliberately excluding the squares! It's not a coterie either, which would imply a limited following by judicious admirers. I think it's more fragmented than that. Rather like the work itself. And maybe that's the problem, if there is one: the vastness of the oeuvre with its many scattered procedures. There's a tendency for big projects to go unnoticed. (I should know.) There are no hit singles. But there is still something radical about montage as *effect*. Whereas the technique is over-familiar, its more radical results are less assimilable. Rancière, as I note in my response to Raworth's processes in *Bad Times*, says we should "put disorder back into montage" (i.e. channel-flipping just doesn't do it) and I think Raworth and Fisher have already done that:

montage in their hands is an inherent challenge to perceptual coherence and narrative modes. Fisher aims for (re-)narrational effects through non-narrative means, which is an exacting poetics. Younger writers apply collage lightly and with a consistency of voice which Allen's work also eschews. Maybe there's something in that? Domesticated collage against its undomesticated varieties? Farther out than Allen: I'm more surprised by the lack of interest in Adrian Clarke, though I recognise the work appears rebarbative toward the reader. Everything torques. He's re-defined the oeuvre in his appropriately titled *Drastic Measures* by revising his old sequences down to one book. (Get it everybody: it's out from Veer.) Ulli Freer has a poetic practice of unceasing process that seems to escape documentation, through flurries of pamphlets and carefully choreographed ritualised performances.

I wondered if you'd care to expand upon the point you make, and which we might include ourselves as part of, about innovative poets moving into education as lecturers and teachers. Do you think this will have a knock on effect in terms of processes, breadth of reading, critical readings and poetics? Do you feel that as a responsibility, perhaps even a weight? Or just as a personal challenge? Do you think this infiltration (if that's not too loaded a word) has happened in a similar way to what has previously occurred in the USA? Is it perhaps disappointing that we have embraced institutional academia instead of perhaps building upon the idealism and utopian visions of the '60s and '70s? Or are we realists or, playing devil's advocate, simply better placed to promote and contextualise our own work whilst paying the mortgage?

There are a lot of questions there, regarding the positions we both find ourselves in, you at Falmouth and me at Edge Hill. It's already had effects, hasn't it, this slipping in through the gates of the academy (and perhaps it has happened in a way not dissimilar to the seeping entryism at the Poetry Society)? A lot of emerging writers are products of writing courses and this is encouraging. A lot of interesting writing is taught and reciprocally interesting writing produced. I feel it as a pleasure that poets (Thurston, cris cheek, Michael Egan, Joanne Ashcroft, Andrew Taylor, Cliff Yates, Matt Fallaize, Alice Lenkiewicz, Mark Smith, and other good writers less visible, like Tony Cullen and Deborah Walsh, as well as fiction writers like Carol Fenlon, Claire Massey, Carys Bray and the late Lisa Ratcliffe) have passed through my tutelage, but I feel my position as a pressure too. You talk about teaching but research is a big part of my work and the *Journal of British and Irish Innovative Poetry* and the critical books we are discussing here, and even this interview, are parts of my research "output"—as are my creative works. I gave a blinder of a reading from *Berlin Bursts* at the Bluecoat Arts Centre in Liverpool last Sunday, and that's a part of research. My collaborations with Patricia and Pete Clarke (and you!) are too. What do I do that isn't research? Unless you can keep the work visible and viable as art and not as "practice-led research" you're no good to your students and no good to yourself. (I'm beginning to feel a certain revulsion to that term and towards phrases like "the creative industries" which is a PR fiction—they are creeping into our professional discourse.) I've written on creative writing pedagogy, chiefly on the necessity of poetics as a speculative student-centred activity, but also on my teaching of innovative writing, but I don't have a very worked-out theory of what I intend to achieve within academia (although I've achieved a lot). I'm proud of the work I did on the Research Benchmarks the HE Committee of the National Association of Writers in Education put together, for example. But perhaps (and here I'm responding to the challenge of Richard Marggraf Turley's introduction to his new edited volume *The Writer in the Academy*) the economic challenges and pressures on the subject over the next few years will bring to the fore the friction mounting between supposed vocational orientations in the subject and art's claims to operate as a critique of society (often by developing forms that directly contest what that legitimising society holds dear). The clash between idealism and drab utilitarianism may still lie ahead. After all, creative writing as an emergent academic discipline has been obsessed with self-definition until now. What do you think?

Yes, it's all research, but sometimes the institution, or specific institutions, may not wish to see it as such. Despite sterling work done by many, including yourself, there is no automatic acceptance of creative work as research. It still has to be framed as research; I don't know how you write, but I don't set myself a theoretical problem to solve each time I write a poem or group of texts. The REF (the government's Research Excellence Framework) may accept one thing, Falmouth may demand another. I've been investigating this framing recently, with regard to my own output—and indeed considering interviews such as this, as well as those where I have been interviewed, along with my critical writing, as proof of research, although I would prefer to see them as poetics. I am perhaps fortunate in that although Falmouth is trying to become more of a research institute it is also very much a teaching institution. I still

Robert Sheppard

greatly enjoy my teaching; I have never particularly enjoyed what we might traditionally think of as academic writing.

With reference to this, and looking back to the time your book covers, what do you see as the product of the 70s and 80s poetics and poetry you document in your book? What individuals, schools or ideas particularly interest you in the 21st century?

This May, I was talking to the author of excellent 9-line sonnets Richard Parker (before his Crater Press won the Michael Marks award) and I was telling him that, in my opinion, he was living through a golden age of avant-garde poetry. He seemed not aware of this. Holly Pester told me when I met her for the first time last week that she liked the historicising of *Bad Times* and I said I hoped younger writers would record their activities. Tim Atkins was saying a couple of days ago that there is a poetry reading on nearly every night in London now—and Manchester seems particularly active with *The Other Room* (run by three fine poets: Scott Thurston, James Davies and the underrated Tom Jenks, whose *A Priori* is both conceptual and funny). I went to the Conversify Conference in Edinburgh during September and encountered not only active younger poets (Jow Lindsay/Francis Crot/Joe Walton and Posy Rider/Samantha Walton, neither of whom seem the least discombobulated by their dispersion of authorial identity) but young academics too (Greg Thomas, Juha Virtanen and Lila Matsumoto), which is gratifying to me as poet, critic and editor. Luke Roberts, Justin Katko, Steve Wiley and Emily Critchley are all active poet/critics. Michael Zand's *lion* arrived fully-formed out of the blue at Edinburgh. Sean Bonney (whose recent work, *Happiness* and *The Commons* is staggeringly good as well as raising uneasy questions) was a plenary speaker. (I've written a response to this, a poem-poetics essay or "manyfesto" as I've called it.) Put with Jeff Hilson's work (*In the Assarts*) and Tim Atkins' 'Petrarch' project (itself a creative writing PhD, note) his two new books look splendid and part of something bigger.

But this doesn't begin to detail the works I'm assembling in a box and about which I felt I might write a survey essay (but which I'm doing here instead, I think). Watch out for David Toms (a great reader), Rachel Warriner and Jimmy Cummins in Ireland. Chris McCabe's *Zeppelins*, and Neil Addison's *Apocapulco* can stand up for Liverpool, along with Michael Egan's *Steak and Stations* and his many other booklets. Simon Perril's *Nitrate* is an excellent take on film history. Zoë Skoulding is giving psychogeography a run for its money in *Remains of a Future City* (my favourite title for a book ever!), and Nathan Thompson is promising work in this area too. Rhys Trimble combines Welsh bardic performance with experimental procedures quite engagingly. Philip Terry's Dante project in progress is more than promising, as is the rollercoaster prose of Tim Allen's *Settings*. Thurston's *Internal Rhyme* is by contrast precise, austere and open. S.J. Fowler's multitude of books awaits me, as does Nat Raha's first volume from Veer. Now I've got to put them all back in the box! This is no scientific selection (I'm aware of younger writers in Sussex and Cambridge I haven't sampled yet, and I'm eagerly awaiting Peter Manson's Mallarmé versions) and I haven't read all of them in any great detail. But I'm excited by this. I need to follow up Sophie Robinson more than I have.

Sophie Robinson appears in two excellent anthologies I think are treasure troves, full of previously un-encountered goodies: Jeff Hilson's *The Reality Street Book of Sonnets* and Carrie Etter's *Infinite Difference* from Shearsman. (The attractions of the innovative sonnet have been absorbing me for a while, not least of all as a writer; I reckon over 130 of my poems take on the sonnet frame in some way.)

Older writers, of course, still produce exciting work (Geraldine Monk's *Ghosts and Other Sonnets* has found its way into this box of mine, with its exacting hauntings and for its having opted for the "innovative" sonnet craze of our day, which I've written about on Pages). Lee Harwood is writing so much less these days, but when poems do appear they are among his best, 'The Books' for example, which was published in *Poetry Wales*. Roy Fisher's *Standard Midland* is a slim volume but has a range leading from the opening meditation on how early man treated death equivocally through to the defamiliarised prose of 'Stops and Stations' which I spoke of at his 80th birthday celebration (the text was published on *Eyewear*). Some of his best works, actually.

I've been casting eyes at the newcomers, not just to write about them, but to allow myself to be potentially influenced by their directions as a writer. Also to see if there's a zeitgeist. (There's certainly a more balanced gender mix these days, as I explain in the introduction to *Bad Times*, which is a very male book.) Clearly, the syntactic play of the language poets has been a road not taken by many. There's a feeling that the wit of Berrigan and O'Hara, Bernadette Mayer and Alice Notley, are important again, and maybe lyric experimentalists like Waldrop and Armantrout rather than Bernstein and Andrews are revered (though there is a strong experimental streak, a draw towards figures like Peter Inman and Craig Dworkin, in the Manchester groupings; there are more writers there than I've listed). All these things are the legacy of earlier work, both British and foreign, but I am both heartened when I see these younger writers working as critics on the poetry of the past (Thomas and Wiley are both working on Cobbing, and included in a special edition of the *Journal of British and Irish Innovative Poetry* Scott and I are editing), but also slightly disheartened by what seems elsewhere like a wilful uninterest in the *history* of alternative British poetries by some writers (such as I predict in my final piece in *Bad Times*, and to which the book is hopefully a corrective). Or they are looking to American work only as if none the things we talked about earlier mattered. Less sympathetically, it's easier to isolate one's genius than to have to admit that the thing has been done before and done better. But maybe this is an evolutionary protection for young writers, I don't know.

Speaking of groups and Craig Dworkin, I've been paying some attention to "conceptual writing" in the US, particularly in the anthology *Against Expression*, edited by Dworkin and Goldsmith. As an anthology— in terms of introductions, headnotes and references to further reading— it is exemplary, but these things also indicate what might be weaknesses in the selected work: the concepts and contexts are often more interesting than the actual texts. Of course, that is mainly the point; the work has a "thinkership" rather than a readership, as Kenneth Goldsmith says. Modes of expression are replaced by plundership (to add my own neologism). We re-write—no, type—the *New York Times* in uniform print, we alphabeticalise the Bible, we erase text to leave only the punctuation, the brand names, the instances of the use of "I". More controversially, we re-narrate the raw testimony of sex offenders (while nodding towards Reznikoff's *Testimony*), we inventorise our possessions or locations, our speech, our food intake (as in the famous Perec piece). We let computer flarf pour out as "poems". We let the computer write random poems with randomised names attached to them (the infamous 7000 page PDF called Issue 1 which contains a "poem" of mine by the way; I get the point: we read the poems in the light of the names. Certainly I've re-claimed "my" poem and I don't experience the outrage of many of the involuntary "contributors"! Indeed, Todd Thorpe in his refreshing review of *Complete Twentieth Century Blues* on *Jacket* likens my work to Robert Fitterman's and others' and I'm willing to see the resemblance if not complete identification). Appropriately, this account is half-description, half-parody. I know you are keen on David Shields' *Reality Hunger* which proselytises (via appropriated text) for appropriation as an aesthetic. I picked up David Toop's *Ocean of Sound* the other day and was interested in how he was noting a similar poetics in the mid-1990s. So it's not new that there's nothing new under the sun! A fact that *Against Expression* emphasises, of course, with its own selective appropriations of Beckett and Roussel.

I've never been more excited and more bored by an anthology than this (but I find my excitement ignored by the assumptions of the anthology, my boredom theorised or re-functioned as "the new interest", as it were)! (That's the opening of another review I need not write.)

I'm currently working towards writing a study of the forms of recent innovative poetries (mainly British but with some international poets), which is underlined by a conception of form itself, that emphasises form not as a vessel to contain its contents, but as a readerly process of forming which is already meaningful, and which brings the text into existence. My approach derives from my axiomatic contention that poetry is the investigation of complex contemporary realities through the means (meanings) of form, embodied in identifiable forms and acts of forming. This implies a test which writing must pass in order to "work": how much does its form trans-form? By this standard some of the inventorising gestures of conceptual writing don't work. The reaction against the syntactic play of the language poets (as noted of British writers too, above) has resulted in an interest in flatness and un-transformation. (Goldsmith reads at the White House; Bruce Andrews never would have.) But many texts do transform their occasions (despite themselves even; Goldsmith talks about the moments beauty and value break through the monotony, a clinamen moment in his theorising which threatens, perhaps by design, to undo itself). The sheer exhaustibility and audacity of Goldsmith's own work, for example, along with his cogent poetics, is touching in some curious way. The racial-political pressure of M. NourbeSe Philip's *Zong!* is chilling (though it is interesting to compare this with D.S. Marriott's take on the "Zong affair" in another fine book missed out from my list above, *The Bloods*. He can form forms!) Peter Jaeger's *Rapid Eye Movement* (in excerpt in the anthology but available as a beautifully designed Reality Street volume) takes on the discourses of dream both objectively and subjectively in two language flows (top and bottom of the page). The anagrammatic play of K. Silem Mohammad's *Sonnagrams*, formed out of the forms of Shakespeare's Sonnets (they are in metre and rhyme!), is astounding (but he is aware of being "poised at an interestingly liminal point between traditionally formal and experimentally procedural conceptions of constraint"). All of these seem transformative texts to me.

The death of conceptual writing (as I'm sure such writers will agree) was inscribed early, a built-in obsolescence embodied by Darren Wershler's millennial *The Tapeworm Foundry*, which is (judging from the anthology) largely a list of alternative "and/or" conceptual experiments that renders the execution of the ideas redundant but nevertheless makes a transformative text out of the exhaustive and even exterminatory processes of his own accumulation and annunciation: "author a sound poem consisting solely of noises made by a spin dryer full of glass eyeballs". That's lovely! These formally transformative works seem to me to be—well—original and creative. I reserve my right to read them against their explicit poetics. My theorising of poetics allows for the element of unknowing or plain self-deception in the things writers tell themselves and each other.

Actually I like Goldsmith's notion of "uncreative writing", though, as an antidote to some of the expressive and therapeutic exercises perpetrated in the name of creative writing but it could also, as I'm pretty sure he'd admit, become yet another optional fixture of that pedagogy if "conceptual writing" appears as Week 12 of an otherwise standard writing module, much as "free verse" still does in some of the worst poetry writing courses. I'm increasingly teaching this work but I'll be severe on lists of abandoned clothes or accounts of how many pints of lager students can drink in a week! Forms and forming: transformation, that's my current mantra.

Phew! Quite a list there. Firstly, your response to Against Expression *is very similar to mine. It's an exciting anthology, but it's mainly the concepts and processes which intrigue me, not the products of them, the texts themselves. It's stating the obvious to say all processes and concepts are only tools for composition, not (necessarily) answers in themselves.*

I'm very interested in David Shields' book, yes—mainly prompted by the way it appears that in music (much as has previously happened to poetry) cultural value has become separated from monetary value. I'm drawn to the late fiction of David Markson and that of other writers who are taking ideas of collage and/or cut-up, the selection and juxtaposition of others' texts, to produce new ones. I've been reading Mark Amerika and others who are approaching this more from the musical idea of remixing: somebody else's version of the original idea. My favourite text of his is a remix of Ad Reinhardt, which managed to re-present the painter's ideas as well as Amerika's whilst discussing 'Why Video Games Suck'. DJ Spooky has written well theoretically about the remix too. More and more I want work to do far more than flag up the way it's made, which I do sometimes find linguistically innovative poetry does. The Norton anthology American Hybrid was ultimately disappointing, but it clearly flags up ways that experimental poetries have fed back into the mainstream. I find myself more and more drawn to authors like Harvey Hix, who I correspond with a little, who clearly have a foot on both sides of the big divide. (He's also very good at finding hybrid forms of creative writing and research—his recent book, Lines of Inquiry, is a fine example of this.) Yes, I'm bored by the mainstream, but I also get pretty bored with the more esoteric textual experiments going on. Cole Swensen, one of the editors of American Hybrid, is one of my current favourite authors. I love the way each of her books works through a different theme or subject, and how she manages to use a multitude of compositional approaches within each of her sequences or series.

The recent anthology Smartarse which I edited, is one attempt to gather together some examples of hybridity. In a rather tongue-in-cheek way I describe it as "post-confessional narrative poetry", but I am genuinely interested in how we can tell stories about ourselves without lapsing into either confession or traditional storytelling. I looked to younger American authors such as Dean Young, Alex Lemon, Josh Bell and Bob Hicok (who is in the anthology) for inspiration and example. Out of the poets I selected I'm pleased to see Nathan Thompson is on both our radar screens. I still regard Martin Stannard as very neglected poet (mainly, I suspect, because he won't toe any party lines), and for me Luke Kennard manages to combine stand-up, surrealism and experiment into something very new and very approachable. He's one of the few writers I know who make me laugh out loud. Steve Spence is an interesting product of both Tony Lopez's Plymouth MA poetry courses (as I am) and The Language Club (which includes Tim Allen and Norman Jope), and I think his two recent books are outstanding. I certainly admire Carrie Etter as a writer and teacher, but many of the names you mention are totally unknown to me, and I am going to go away and seek them out.

The Reality Street Book of Sonnets is indicative, for me, of a current interest in the renewal of traditional forms. My students who take my Poetry & Form unit are drawn to ways of writing where they can see a lineage and understand the reinvigoration of a form. They understand all forms are constructs, but they still like having a form to start with when they come to write. The sonnet is always popular, and I have also had a very good *response to prose poems from Ann Killough's* Beloved Idea *where she explores the idea of metaphor at some length. Rusty Morrison's* The True Keeps Calm Biding Its Story *is an interesting and inspiring exploration of fragmentary communication using an idea and form rooted in the telegram, an outdated means of communication if ever there was one. I'm interested too in what Tony Lopez is doing with his collaged prose, which gets rawer and rawer as each book gets published. I haven't got a handle on it yet, but it's engrossing.*

I continue to read David Miller's Spiritual Letters *project with interest as he continues to try and answer the question of how one writes of faith, doubt and belief in the 21st Century; S.A. Stepanek's* Three, Breathing, *a long poem published by Wave Books, is another attempt to answer the same question. David Grubb's work in this area also continues to intrigue me, sometimes despite critical reservations I hold—I find myself moved anyway.*

The prose poem continues to intrigue me, as does collaborative writing. I've just published a new chapbook with Paul Sutton, which draws on film and the concept of place, and Nathan Thompson is editing the third collaboration we have undertaken ready for future publication. I remain very interested in ekphrasis and how we might write about the visual arts. John Taggart's Rothko sequences remain an inspiration and delight in this area. I confess though that at the moment I find myself far more interested in creative nonfiction, and contemporary music & writing about music than much current poetry, mainstream or otherwise. Perhaps working through your list will give me some new ways of thinking about things, and rekindle my enthusiasm? I hope so.

Who knows? That looks like a pretty sound list. Miller, yes. Markson I should look at, if only from my Malcolm Lowry obsession. It's funny. It's a bit like our maps of London: they are geocentric. My list has a number of North West names on it; yours has a South Western bias. Nathan's on both lists not just because he's a promising writer, but because he commutes between the two areas (via Jersey!). More seriously: it's great to see it. And good to see your own various creative projects—the prose poem, collaboration, writing about aesthetic visuality—flagged up there (whether they end up being "research" or not). I'm particularly interested in your collaborations (particularly as we did one!). What is your poetics of collaboration?

Collaboration, for me, usually combines a process with a dynamic that arises from constantly being surprised where the collaborator takes the sequence or series. Sheila Murphy gave a fantastic talk at an Arvon residential we ran together about trusting the process and the other person[s] involved. It's difficult to talk about the idea of a third voice resulting from two poets collaborating without sounding mystical, and disappointing that most theory concerning collaboration comes out of business models rather than creative practice.

I've undertaken 16 written collaborations since 2000, not including writing/visual arts crossovers or painting projects, so it's a major part of my output these days. I'm simply the sort of person who enjoys setting something up and following it through, and one way of getting to know other writers is to work with them. The initial work simply gets done, and then debate happens around editing, shaping and publishing.

I did approach a publisher regarding doing some sort of selected collaborations book, but they decided the texts weren't experimental enough for their list! Maybe it's best to leave it in pamphlet & chapbook form, or scattered throughout cyberspace.

Of course, my poetics of collaboration might also be seen to include technologies themselves, usually email as a way to facilitate the collaboration. Many of the sequences are also subject driven, for instance the recent Voiceover (Riverine) *with Paul Sutton deals with films, cities, psychogeography and rivers as both a subject but also as questions: how do we remember films, how do imaginary and real cities compare, how do films change our perception of a city? And, of course, how exactly do we write about those things—is there a "suitable" form to be found or invented? How do two versions of the same place—namely Paul's version and my version—co-exist in the same poem?*

These are of course questions that arise from the work rather than precede it. The work doesn't necessarily answer them. Does your work emerge from subject matter or does that emerge as you grapple with a form? I know you sometimes allude to images or other writers?

I've mentioned the prose piece dedicated to Sean Bonney that I read at the Bluecoat last week. It's "based" on Milton's first sonnet 'To a Nightingale' and I plan to use all 24 of his sonnets in some way. I'm toying with the title (ripped off from the Chapman Brothers I know) 'Bad Poems (or Sonnets) for Bad People'. I have a number of conflicting poetics problems: how to put disorder back into collage, whether to make rebellion slow and thoughtful, how to listen to the world as an aesthetic, how to progress the polystylistic, polyformalist work I seem to have pursued in recent sequences, while trying to return to centripetal, entropic forms (after the centrifugal lyricism of *Berlin Bursts*), how to encode human unfinish in new ways. How to deal with the structural immiseration engineered by the present government. (I've heard a number of younger writers, who can't remember the 1970s and 1980s, saying that perhaps this will be an era when bad times will again make for good poetry. In that modern parlance, I'd say to them: be careful what you wish for. I want—unjustifiable utopianism is seeping through, I know—good poems (or Bad Poems even, given my possible title) to make good times.

However, as I wrote in my latest journal entry: "These poetics ideas are not ideas for poems." I seem to be producing a series of "anti-biographical" texts, and I have just finished another of those, but that's looking back. I've just finished, or think I've finished, my "fictional poems" (the supposed effusions of the bilingual, dual-oeuvred Belgian poet René Van Valckenborch) and would like another shot at that particular idea (with another Creature), as well as picking up on some of the ideas he had. To let myself be "influenced" by his poetics, by his conceptualisations of space, for example. (That may sound absurd but it doesn't to me: the project was partly about writing what I would not have done over my own signature.) But I'm very perverse about poetics ideas (a perversity I've taken cognizance of in my critical work on poetics, even in my remarks about the conceptualists earlier): one day I write something about eschewing the autobiographical or conceptualise "becoming as invisible as a professional translator", as David Lehman says of Ashbery, and the next day I do the opposite! I give up sonnets and then start a new sequence. Issuing permissions to continue through negatives. Textual disobedience.

[*Stride*, 2012]